GARDEN GNOMES HAVE ISSUES

GREG STONES

CHRONICLE BOOKS

SAN FRANCISCO

Huge thanks to Brooke (the best wife ever), Steve Mockus (the best editor ever), and Michael Morris (the best designer ever).

Library of Congress Cataloging-in-Publication Data available.

ISBN 978-1-4521-4475-7

MIX
Paper from
responsible sources
FSC™ C104723
www.fsc.org

Manufactured in China

Designed by Michael Morris

10 9 8 7 6 5 4 3 2 1

Chronicle Books LLC
680 Second Street
San Francisco, California 94107
www.chroniclebooks.com

Special quantity discounts are available to corporations and other organizations. Contact our premiums department at corporatesales@chroniclebooks.com or at 1-800-759-0190.

GARDEN GNOMES HAVE ISSUES WITH . . . .

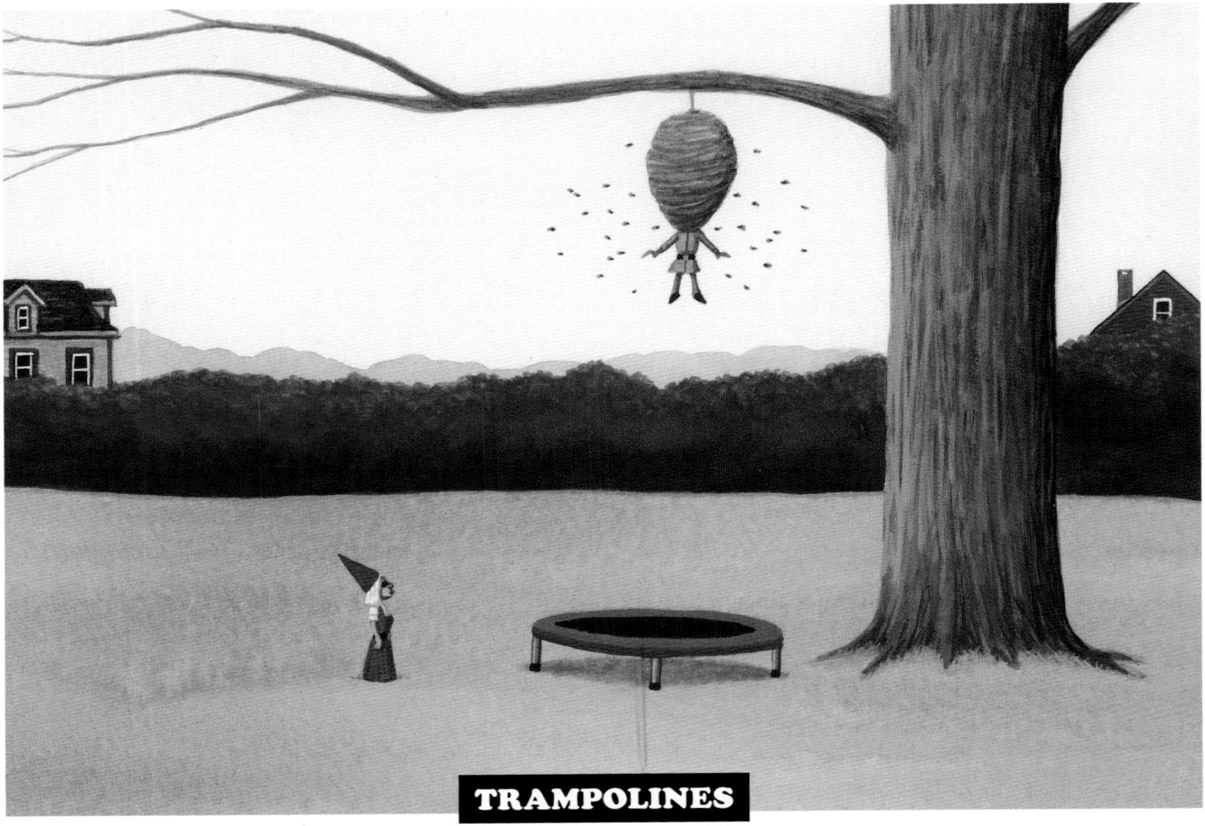

TRAMPOLINES

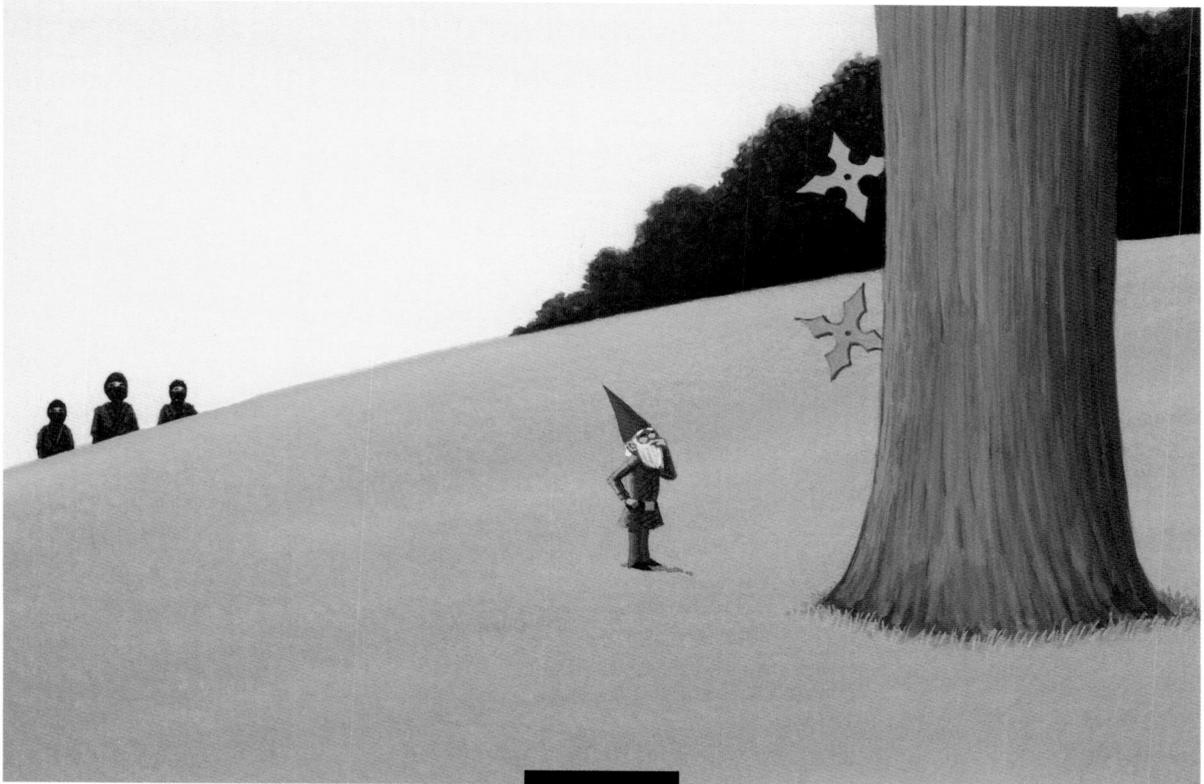

NINJAS

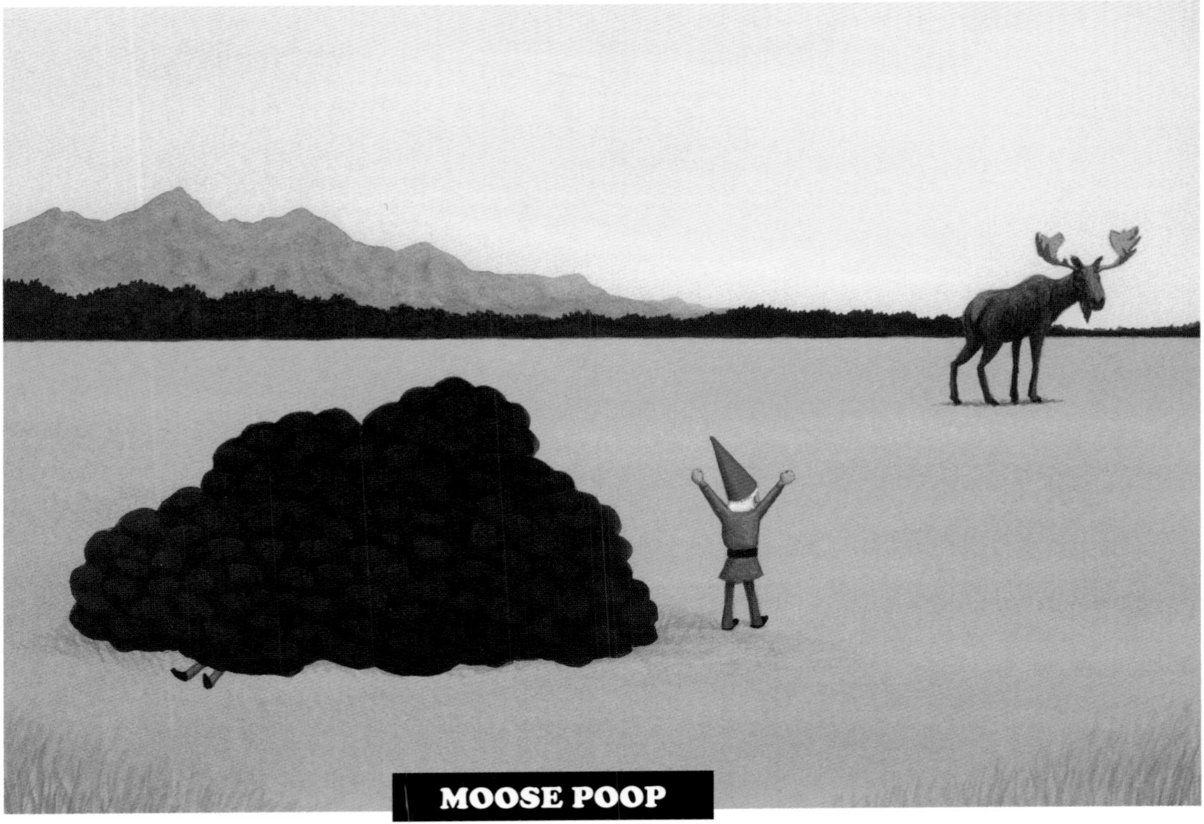

MOOSE POOP

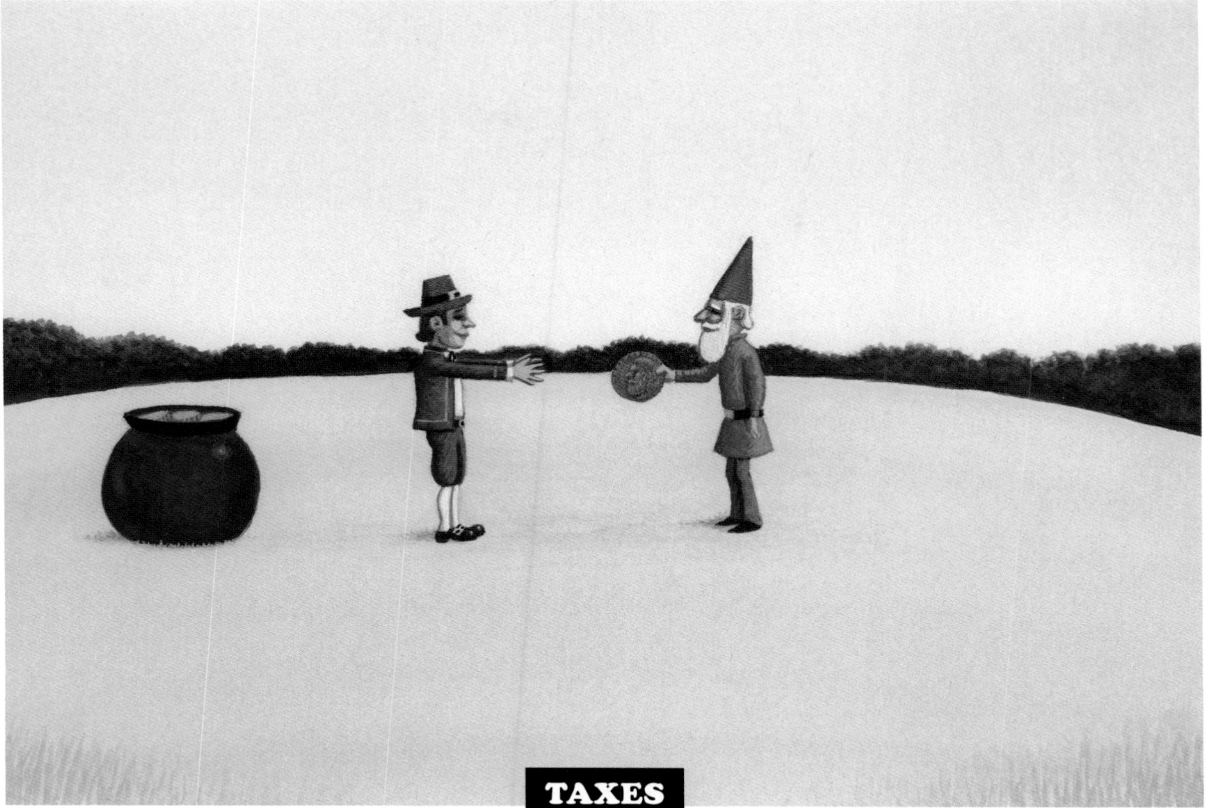

TAXES

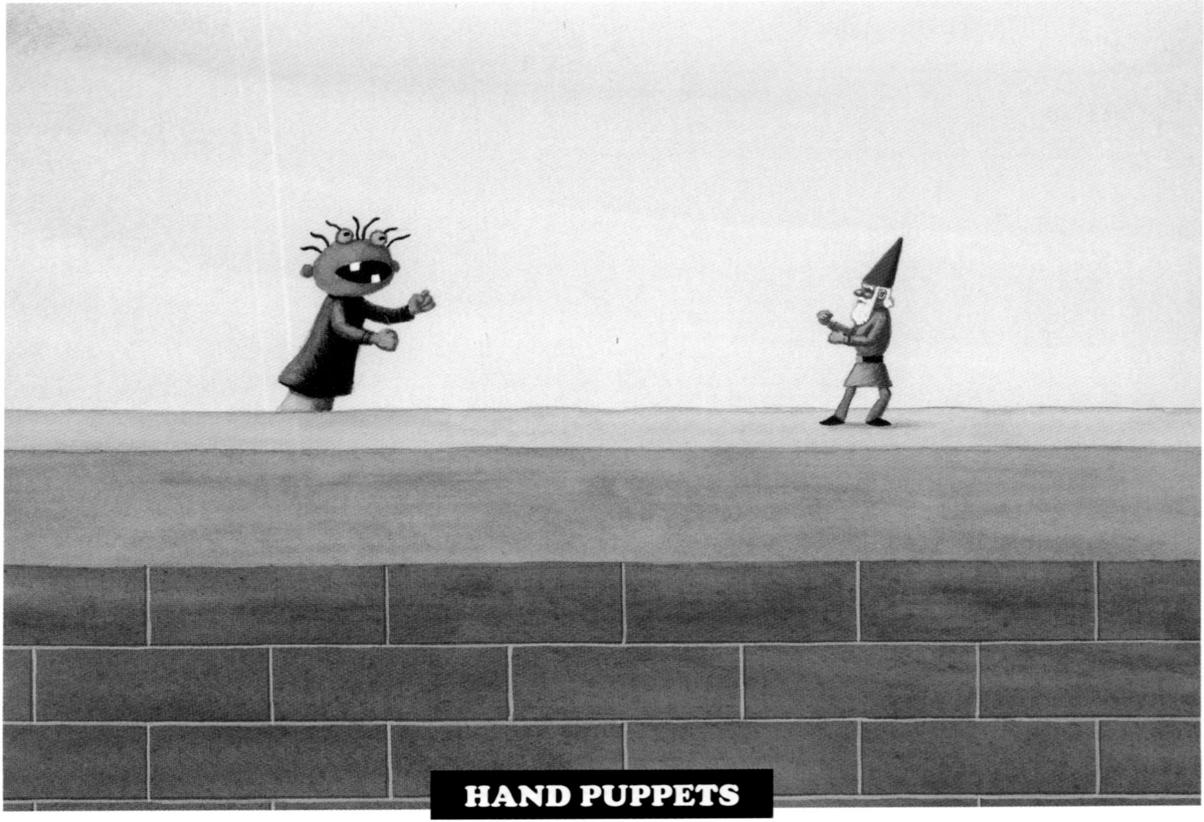
HAND PUPPETS

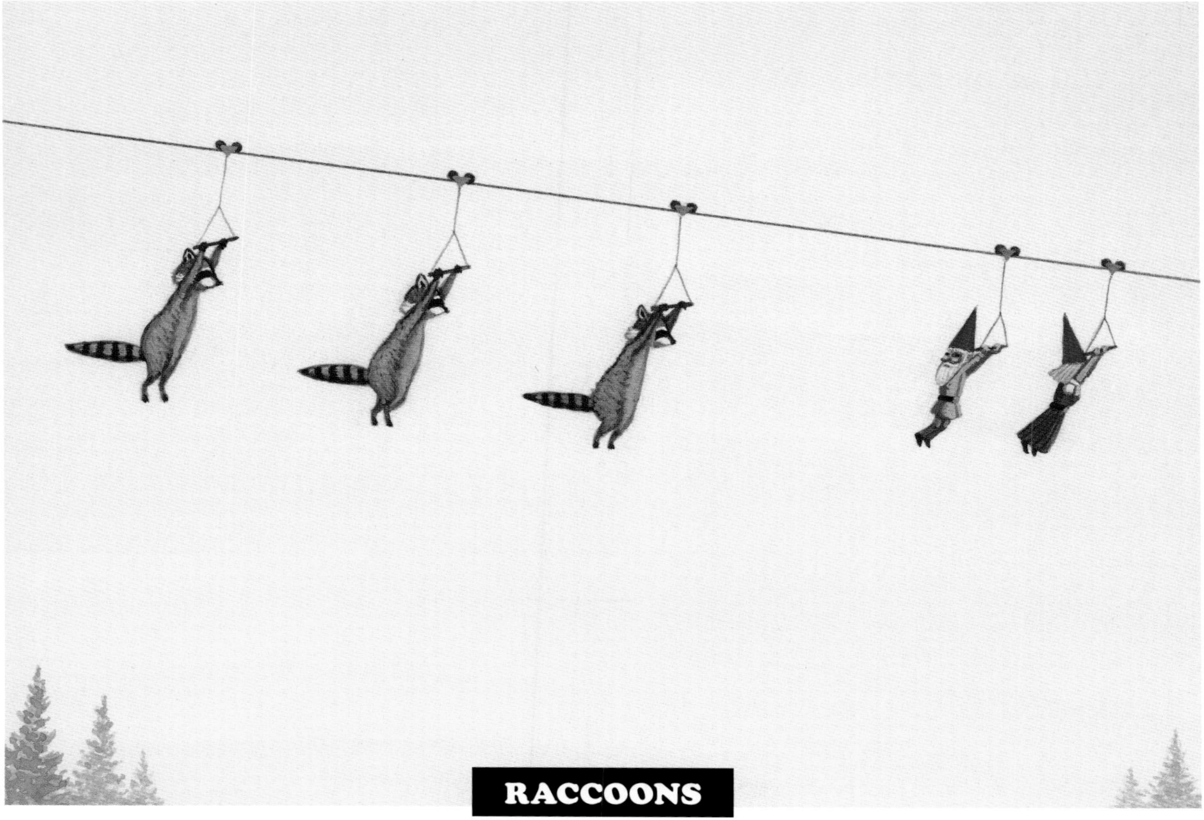
RACCOONS

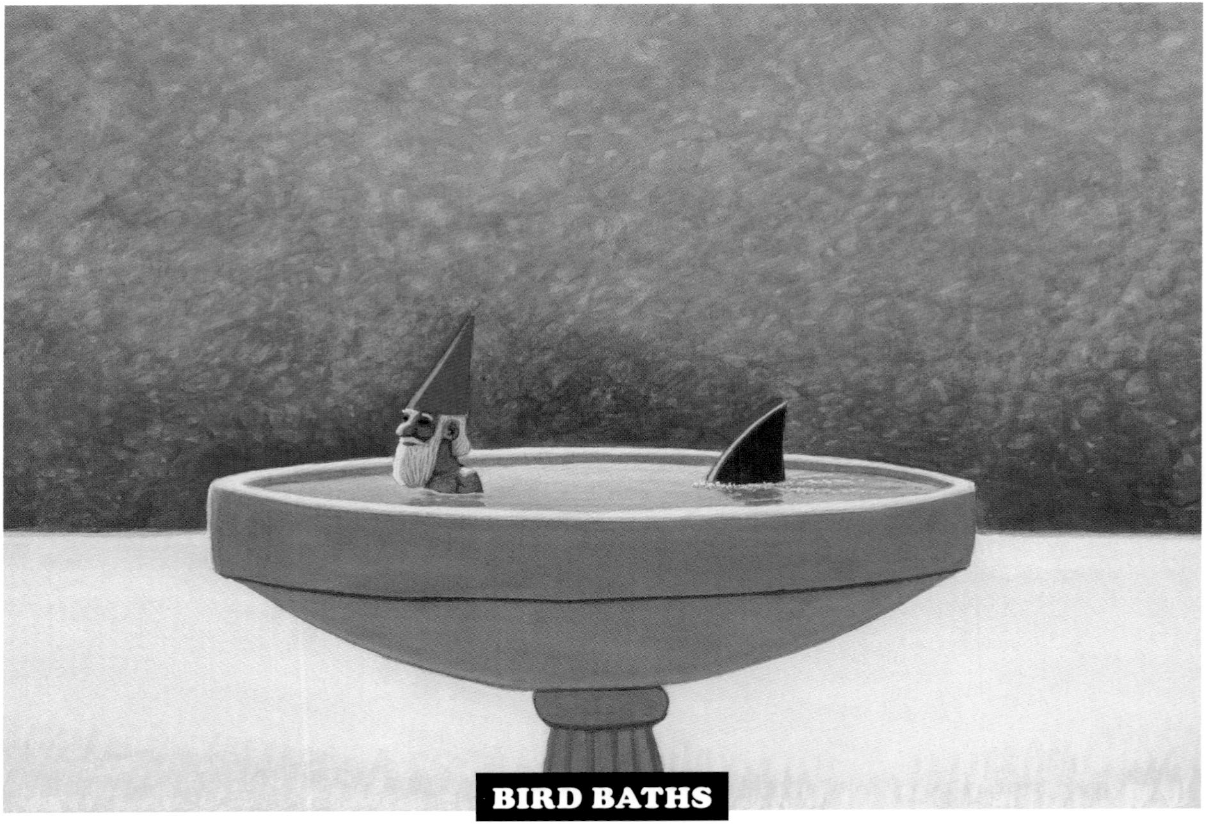

BIRD BATHS

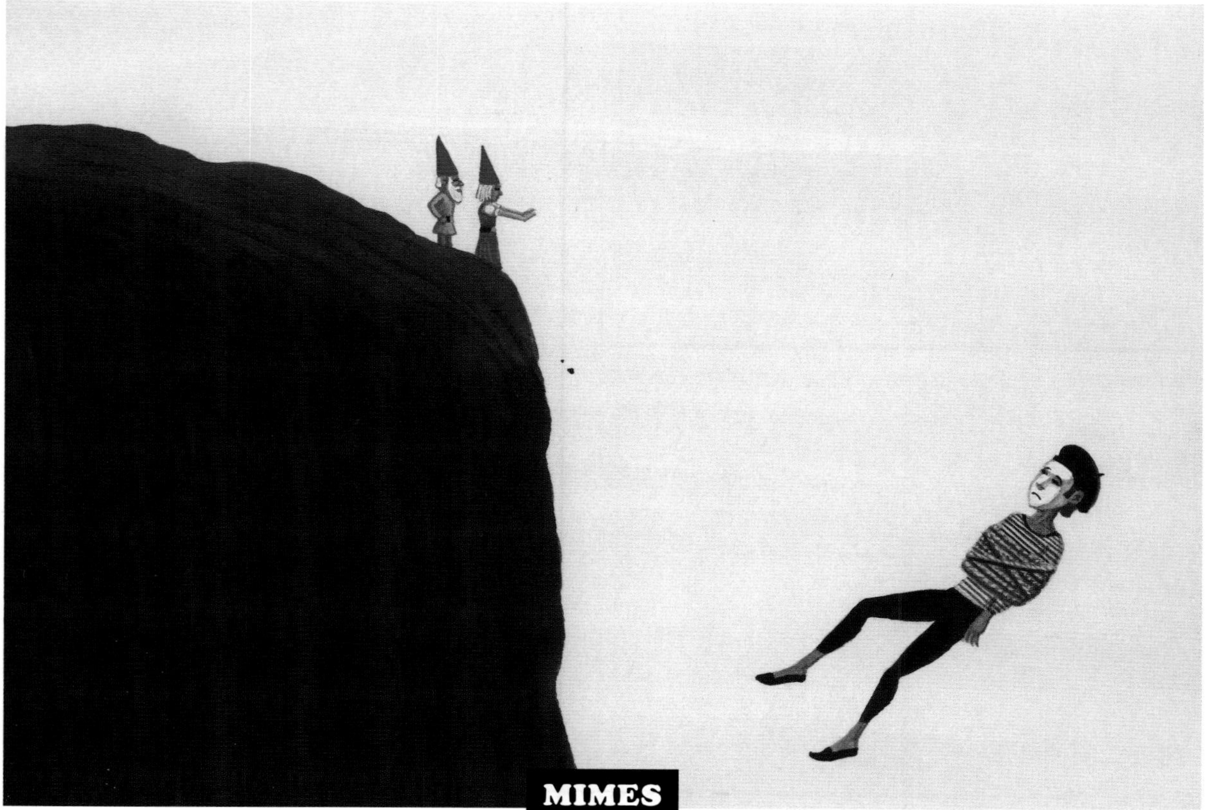

MIMES

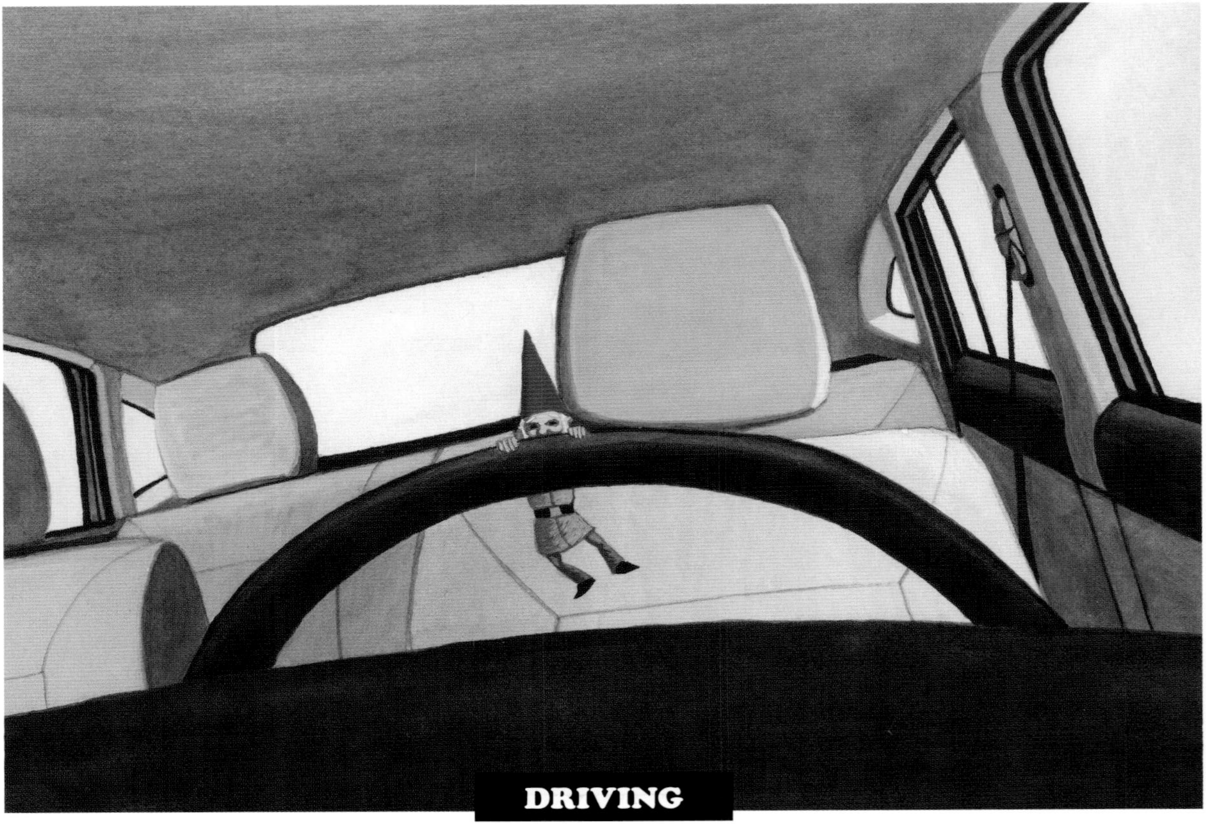

DRIVING

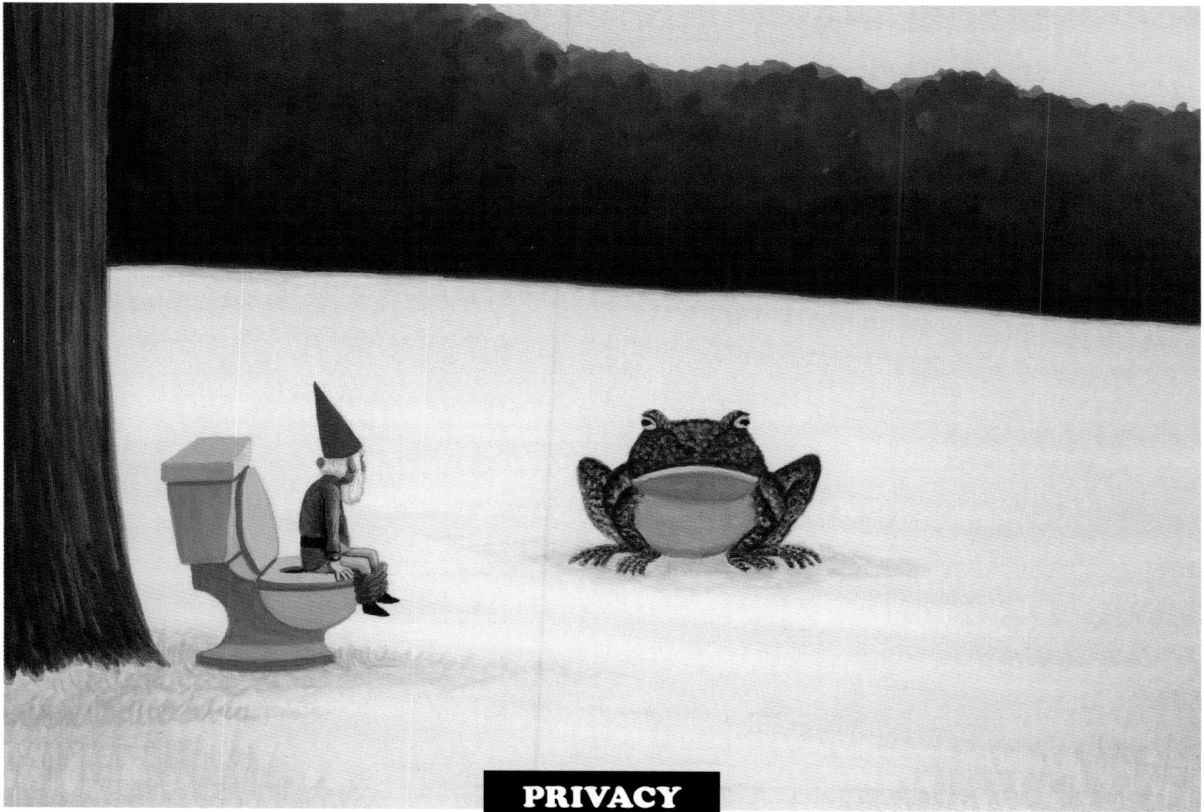

PRIVACY

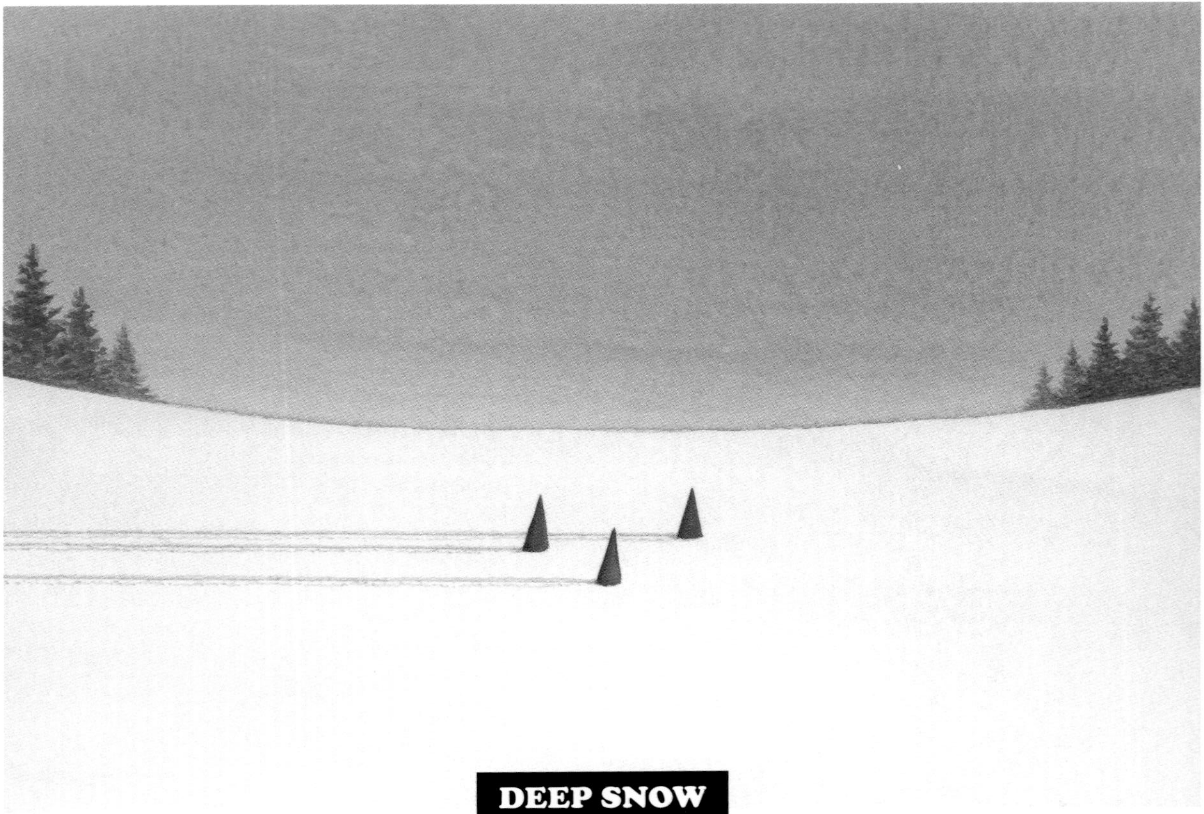

DEEP SNOW

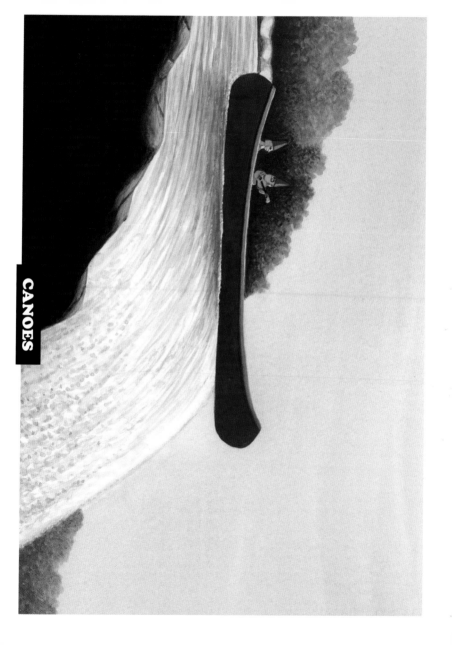

CANOES

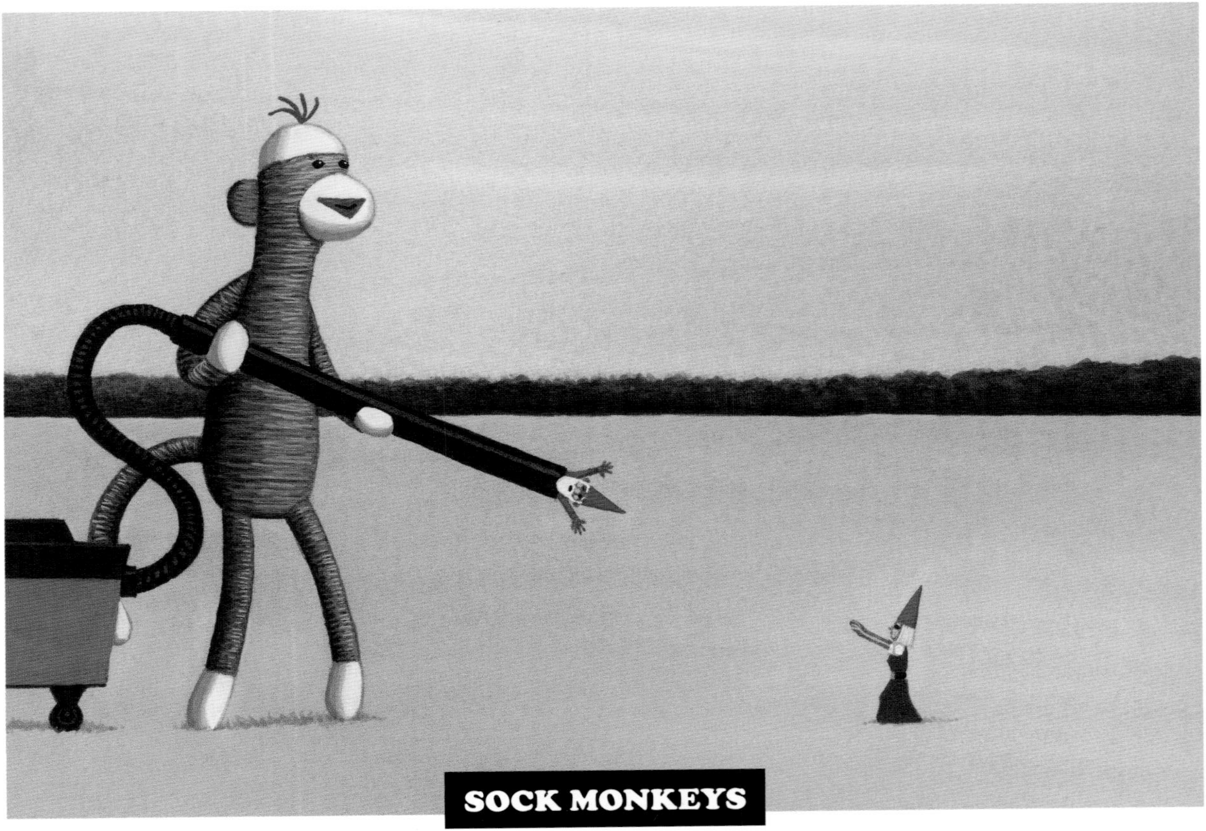

SOCK MONKEYS

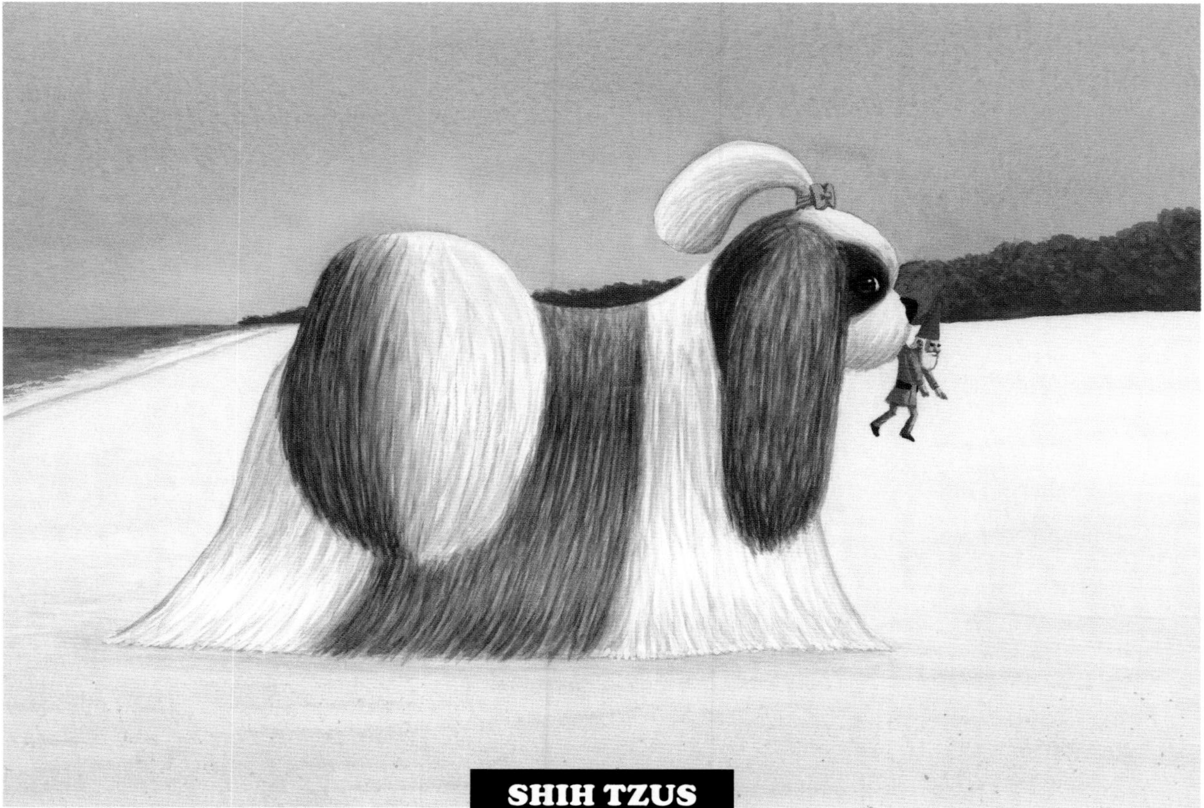

SHIH TZUS

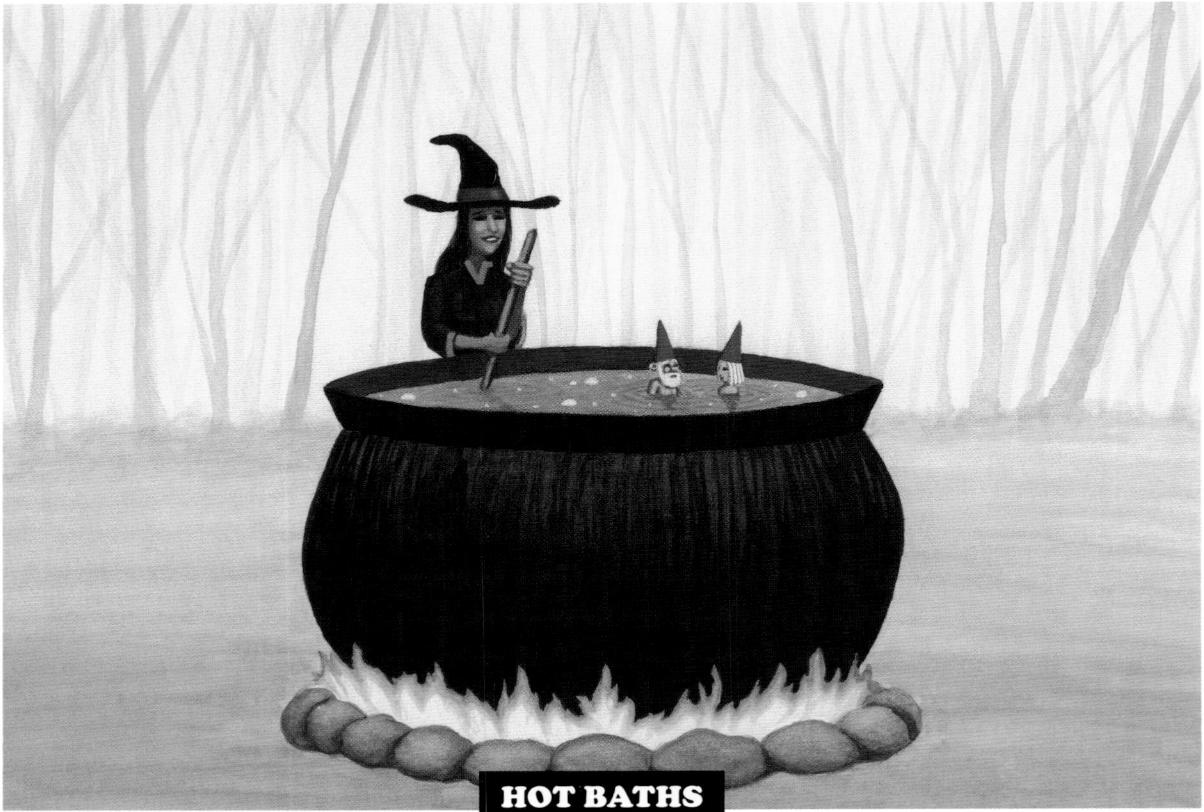

HOT BATHS

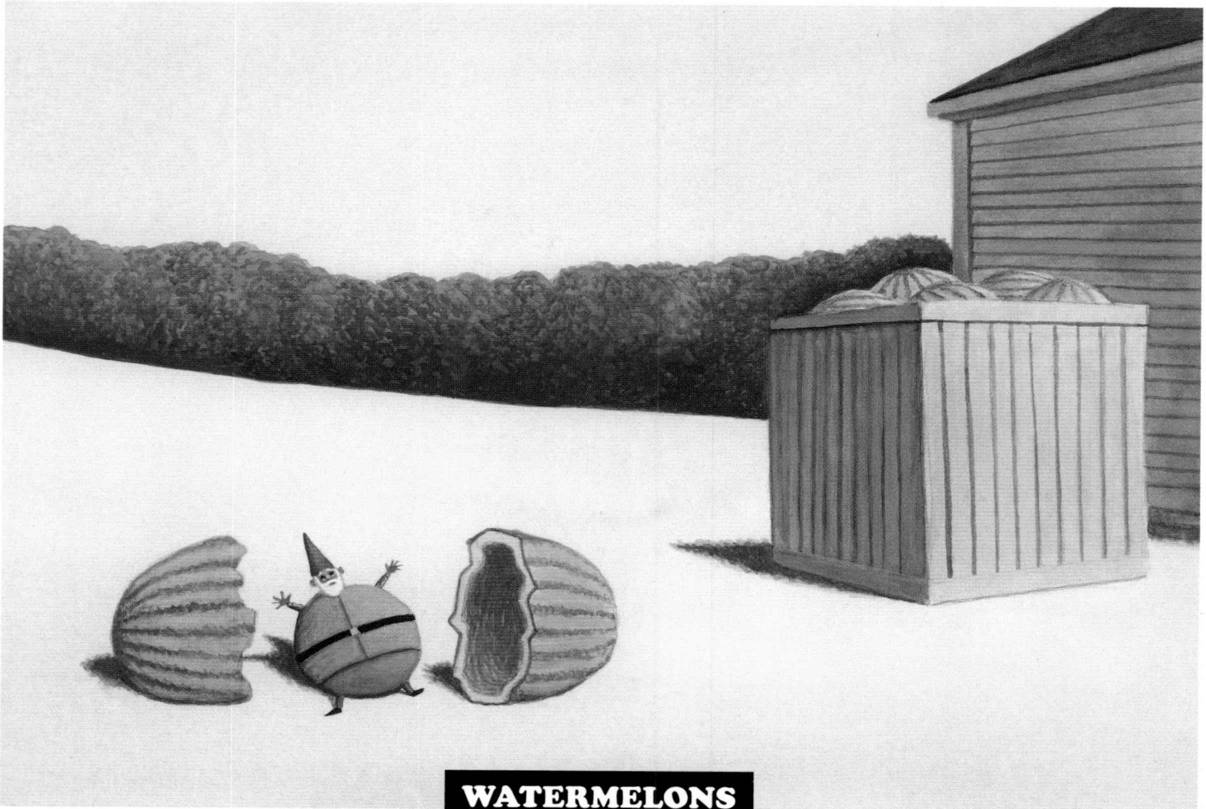

WATERMELONS

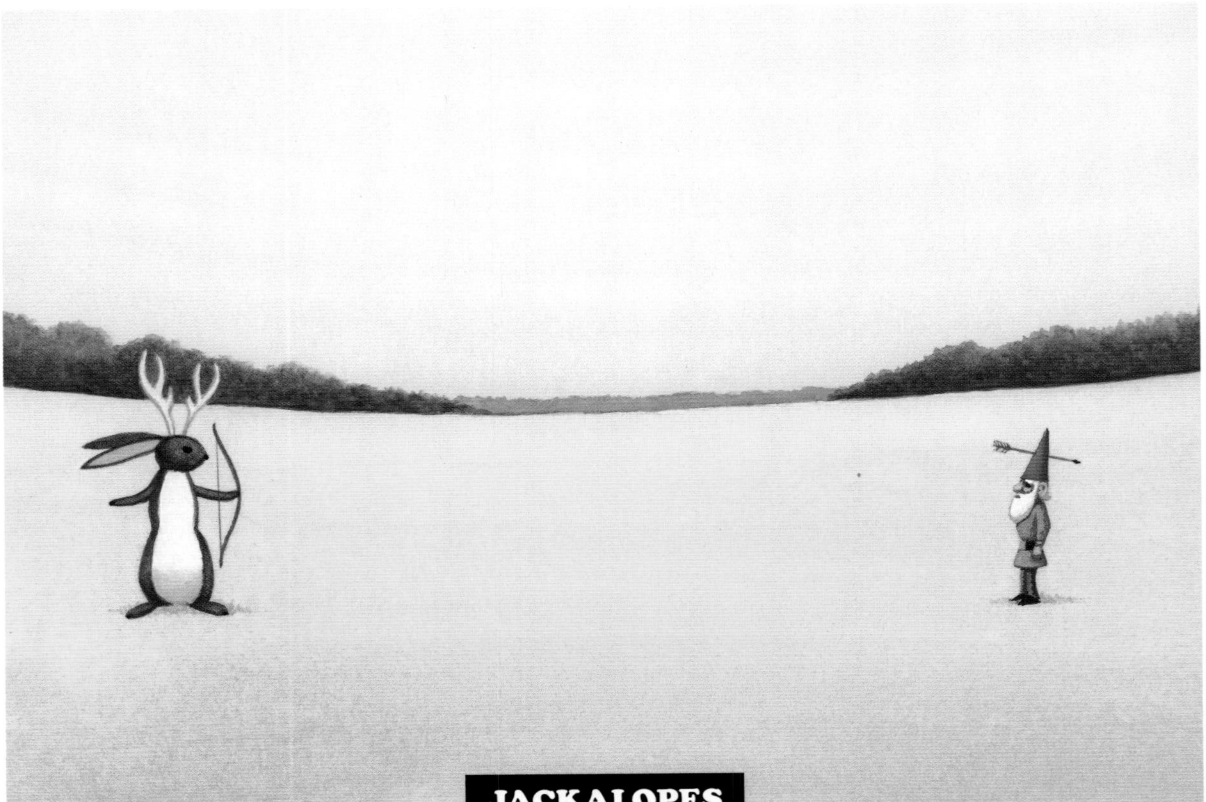

JACKALOPES

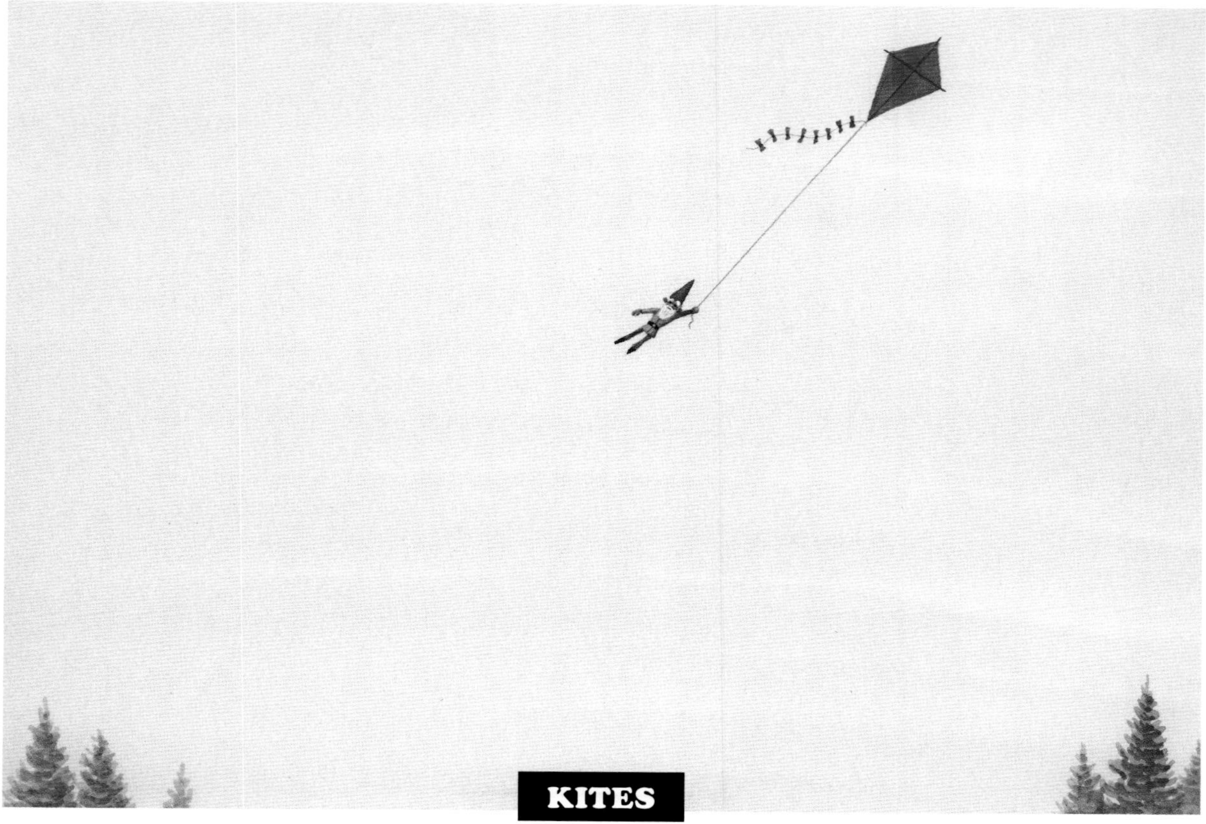

KITES

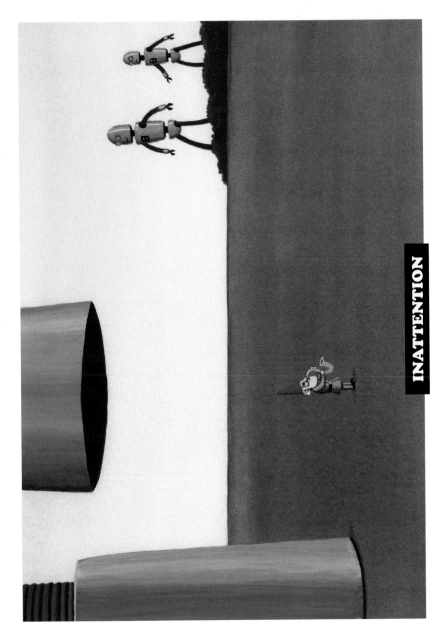

INATTENTION

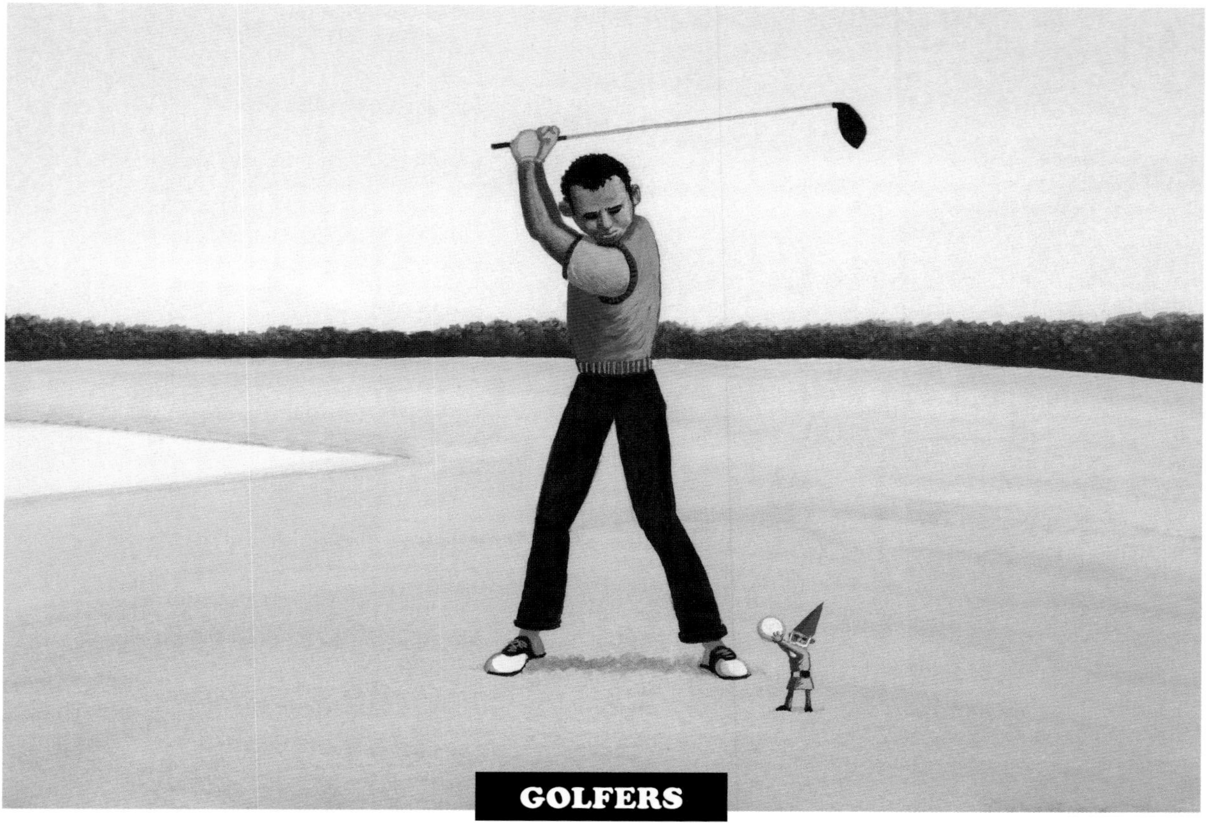
GOLFERS

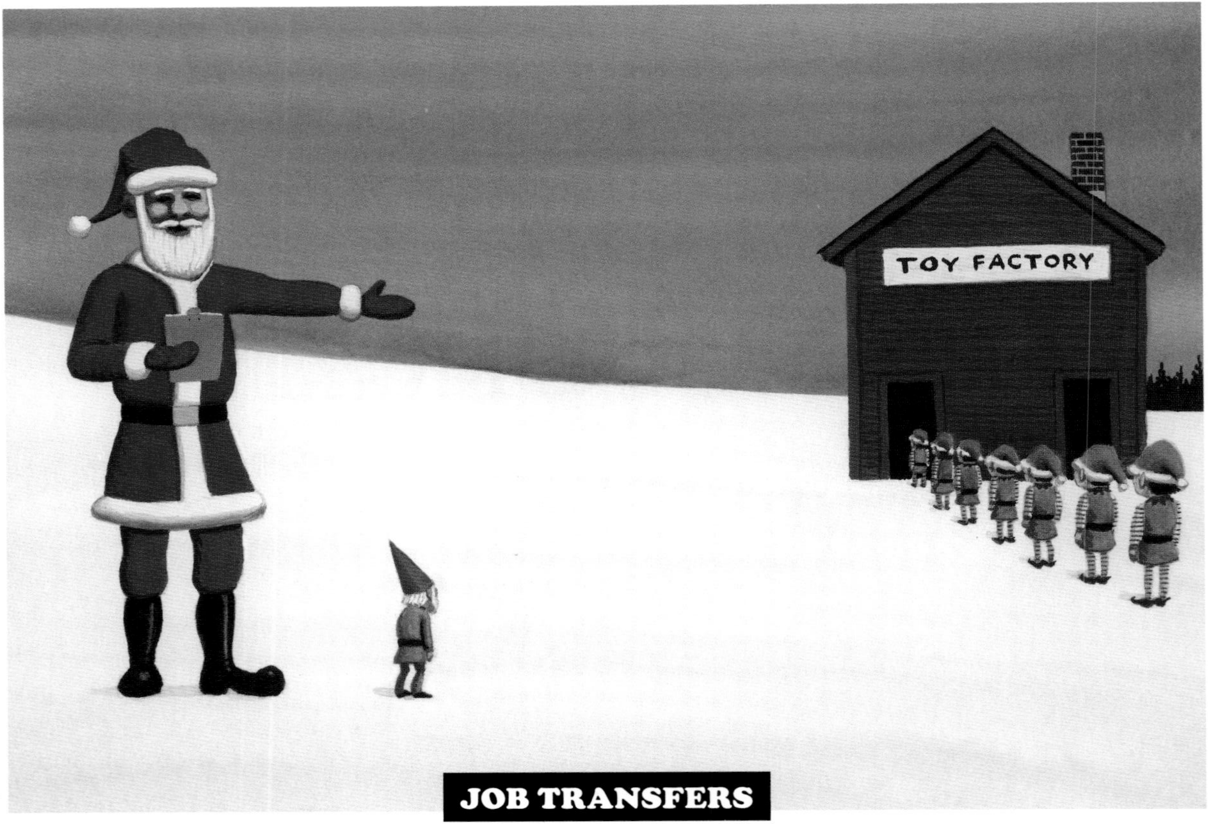
TOY FACTORY

JOB TRANSFERS

GARDEN GNOMES REALLY ENJOY . . .

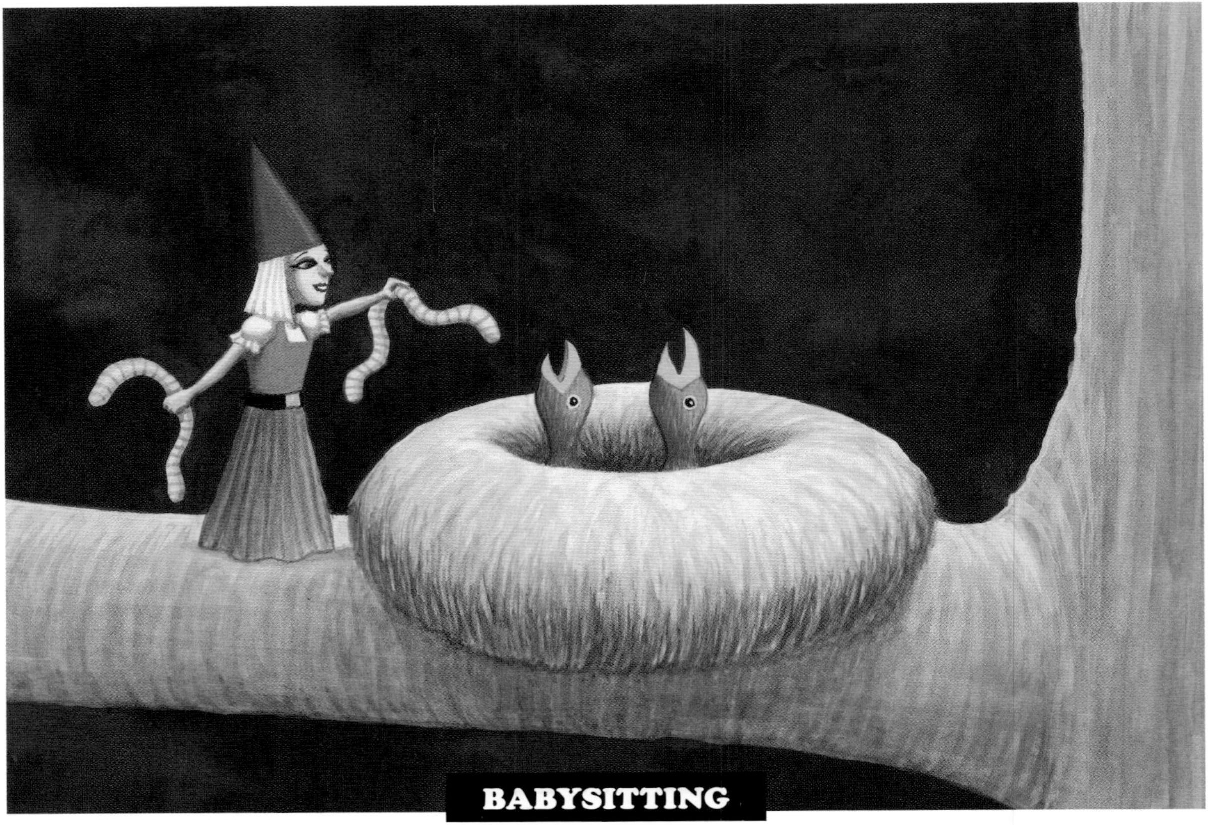

BABYSITTING

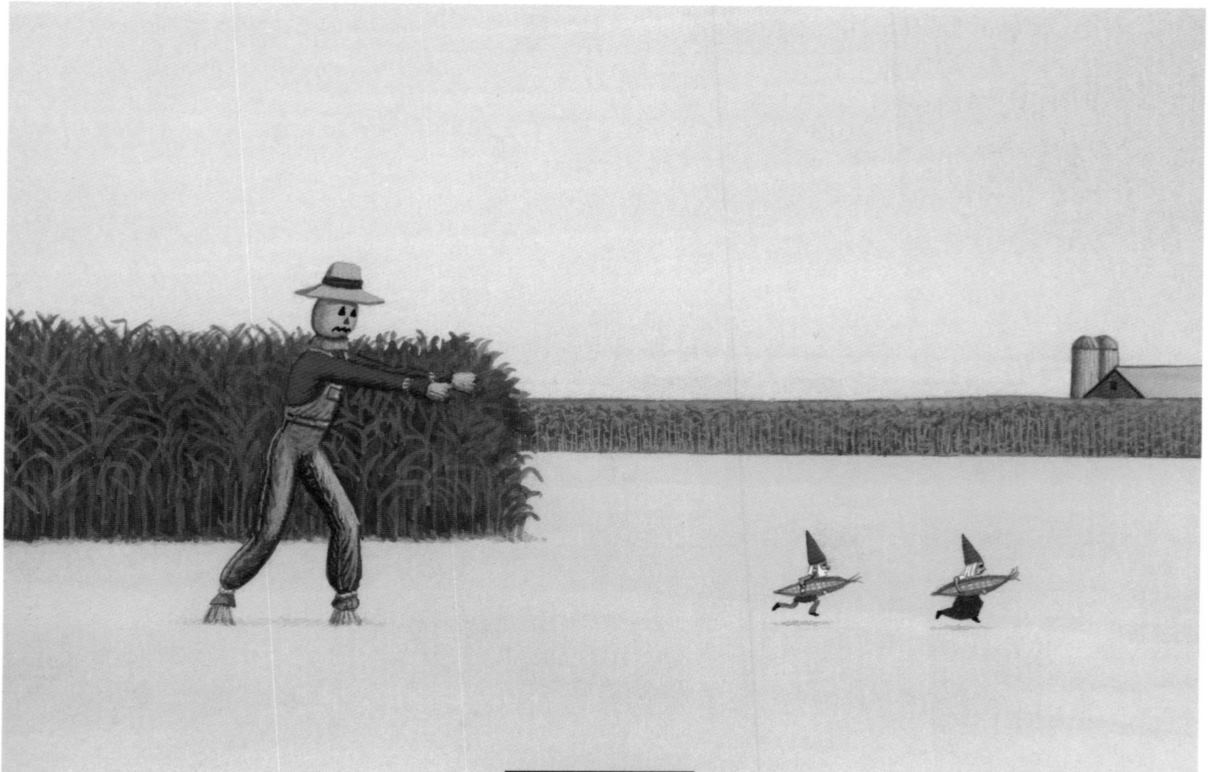

CORN

PAPER AIRPLANES

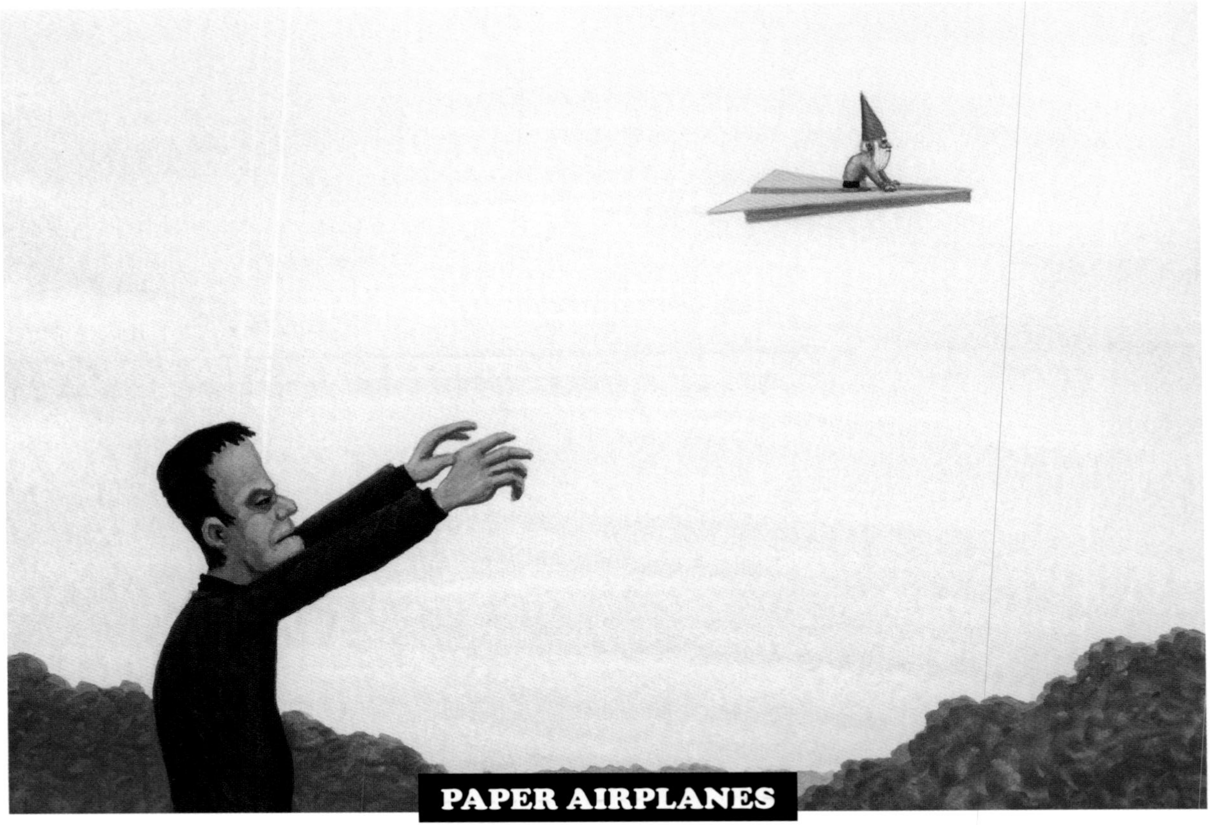

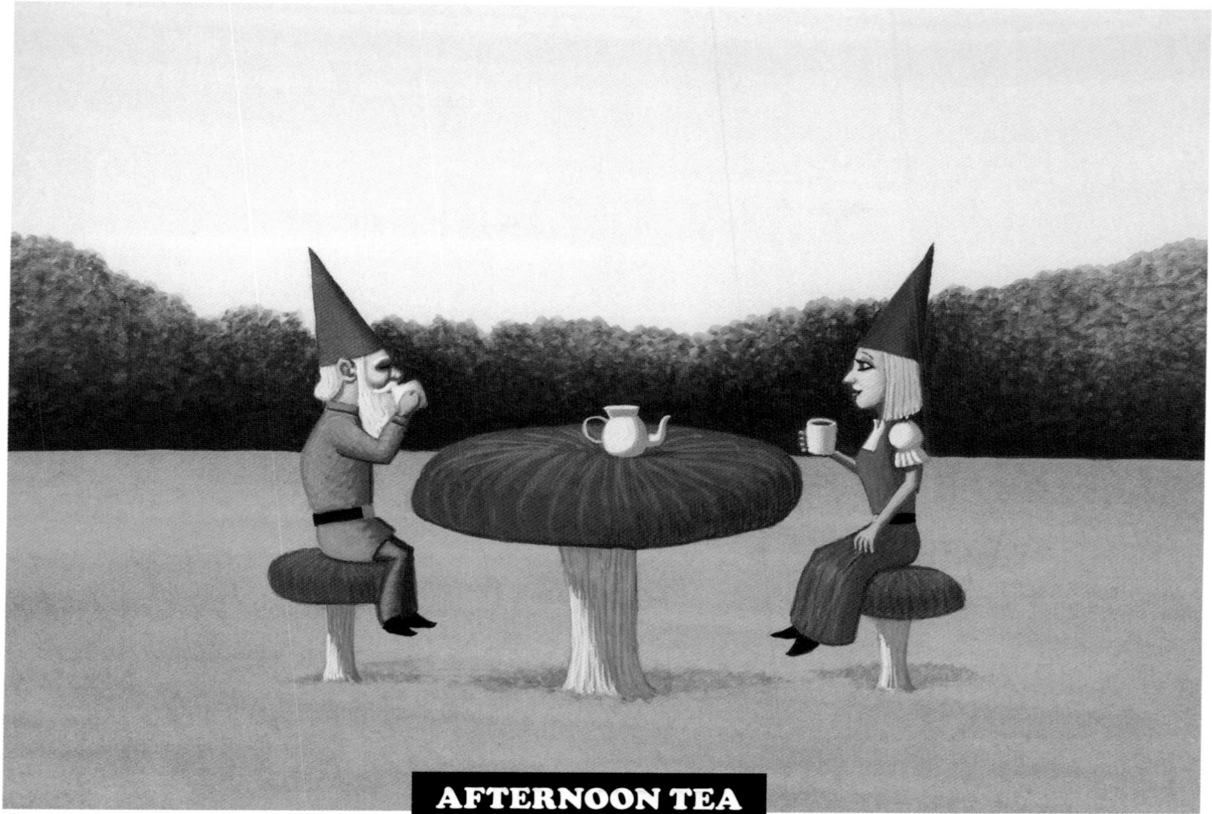

AFTERNOON TEA

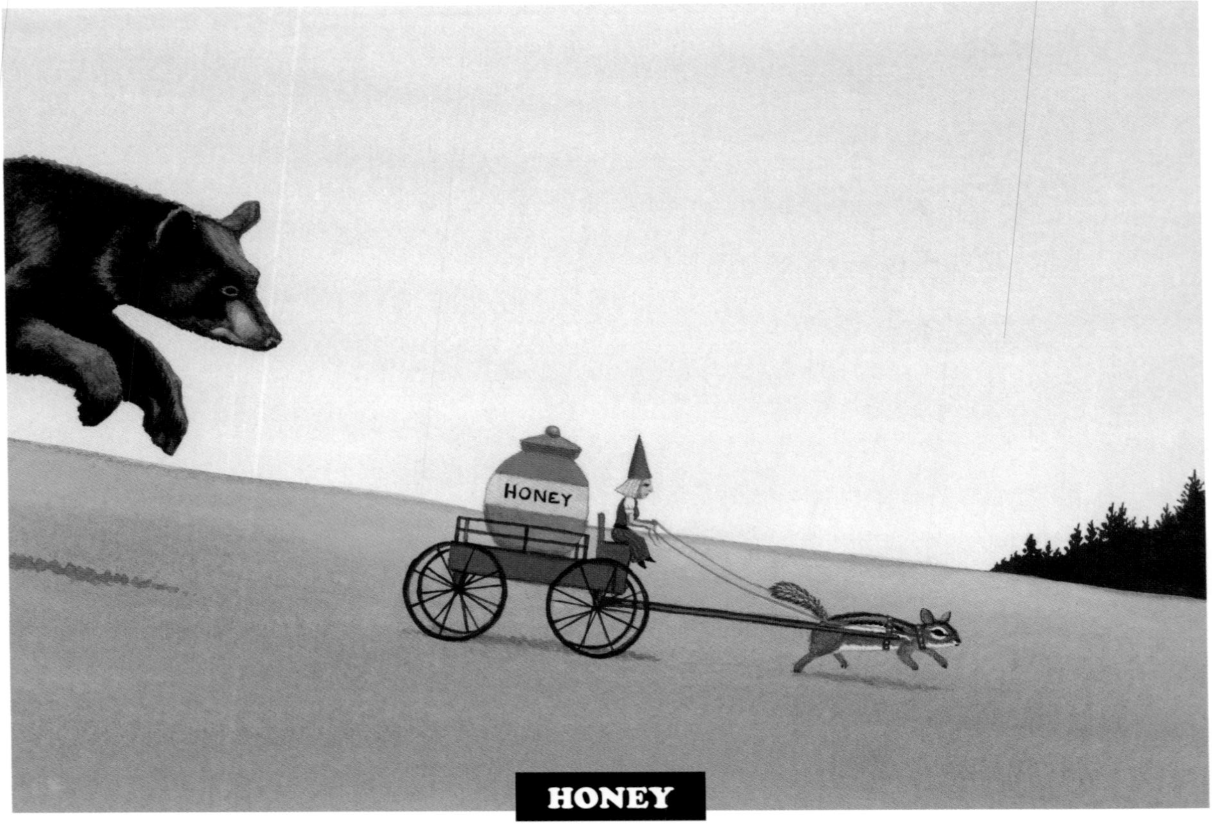
HONEY

HONEY

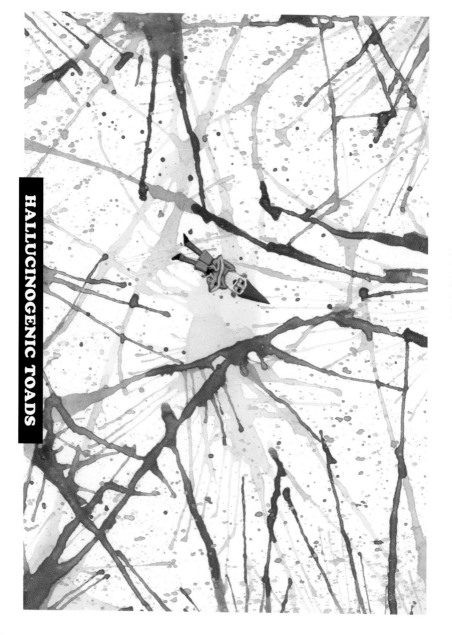

HALLUCINOGENIC TOADS

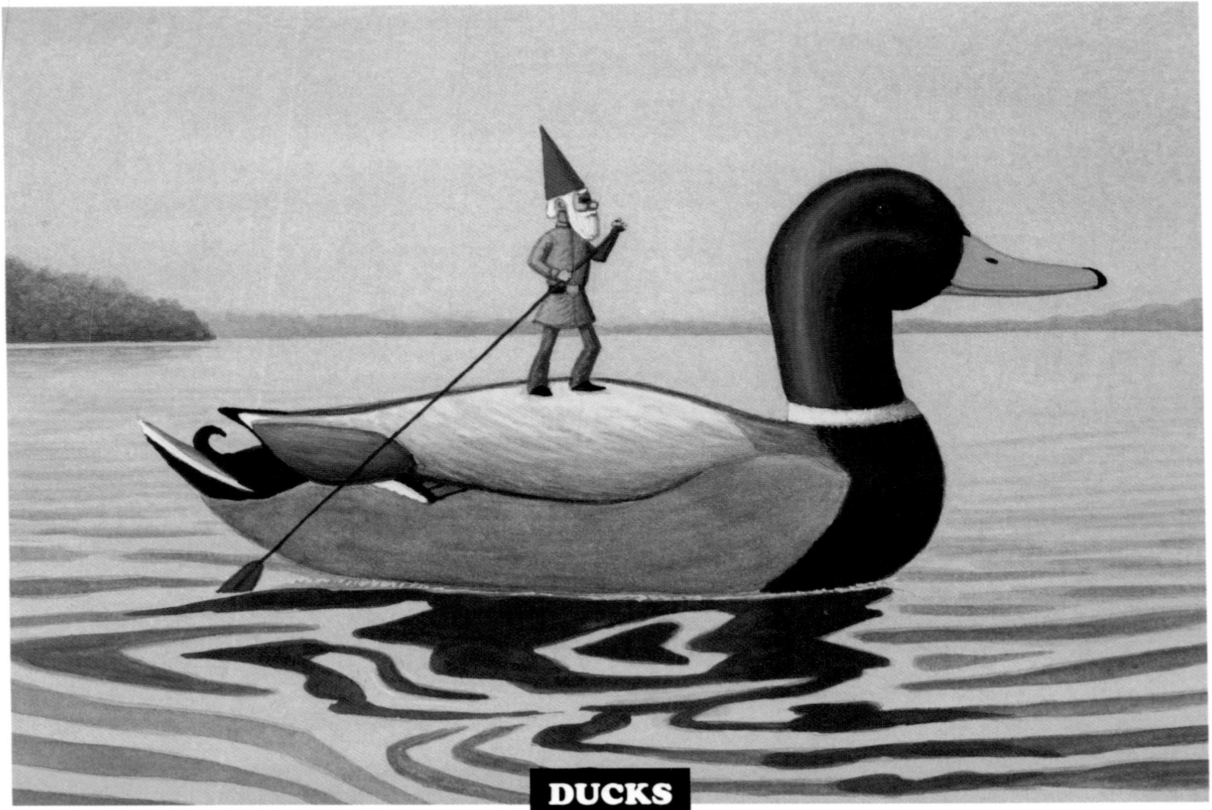

DUCKS

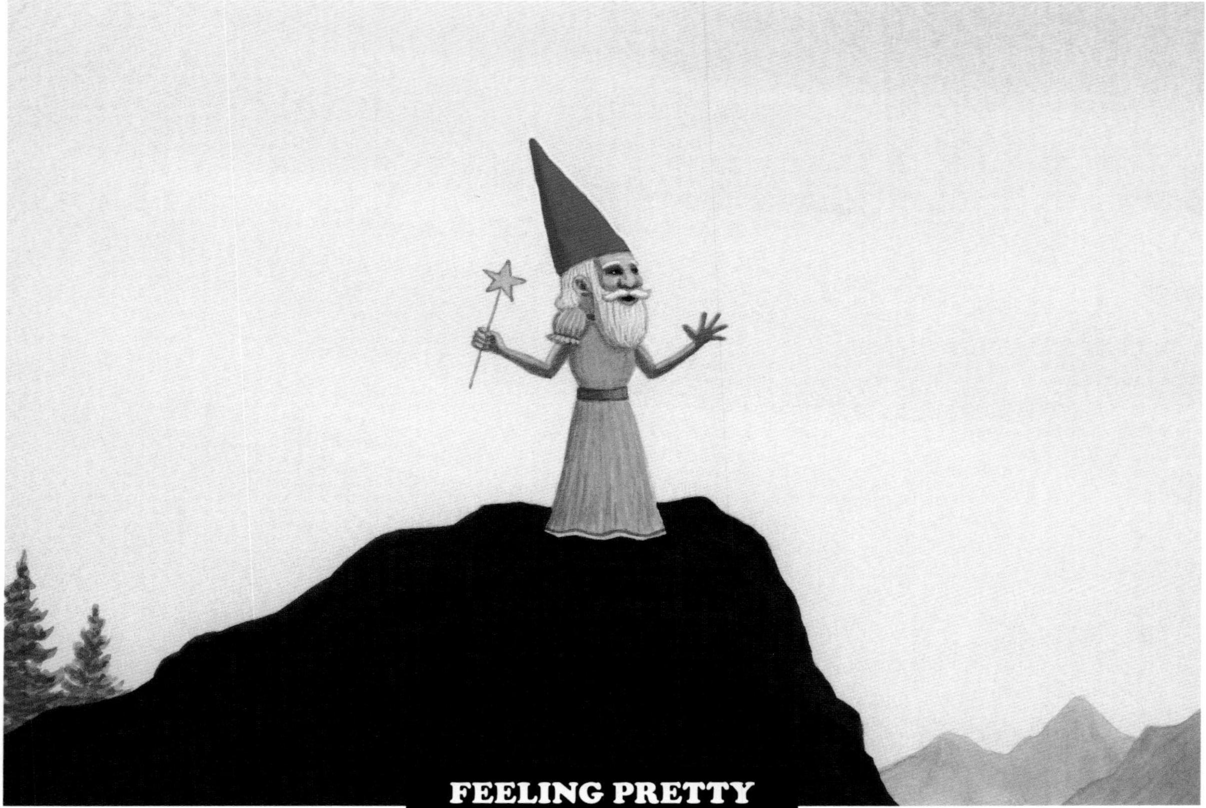

FEELING PRETTY

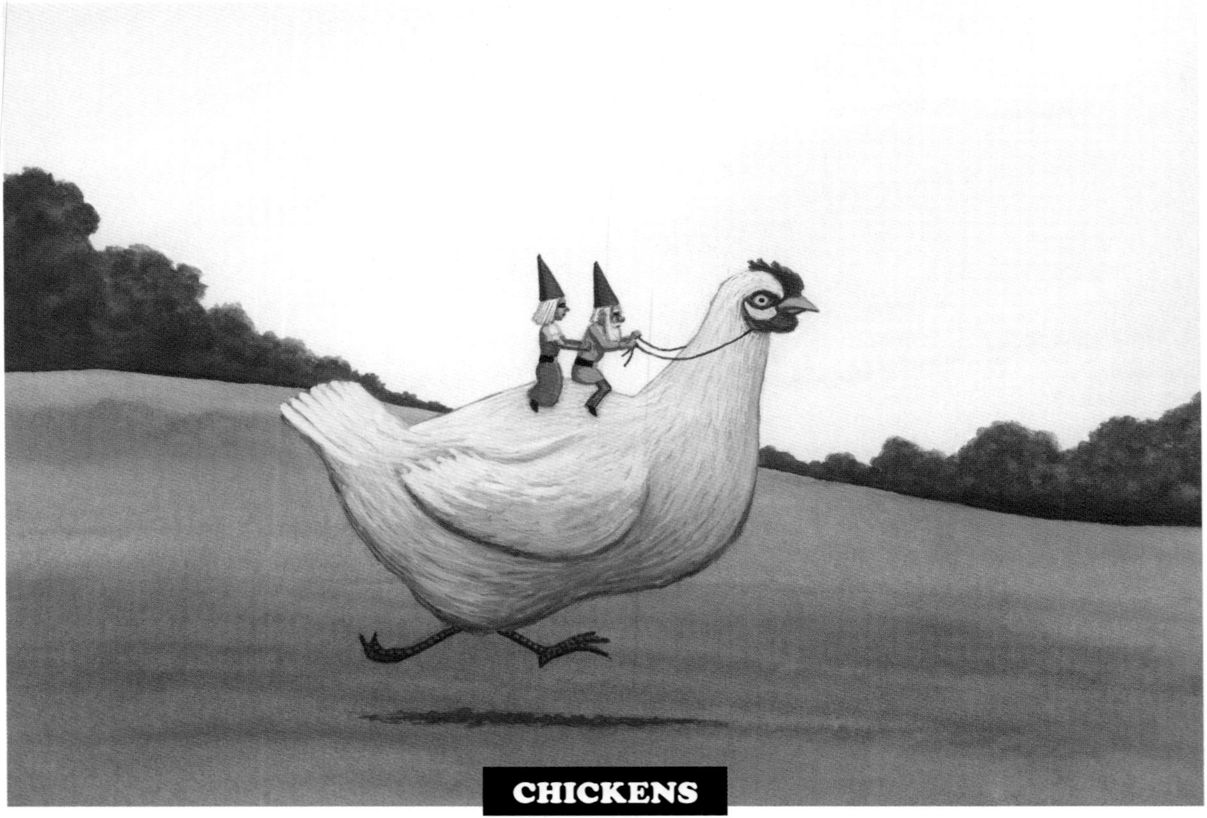

CHICKENS

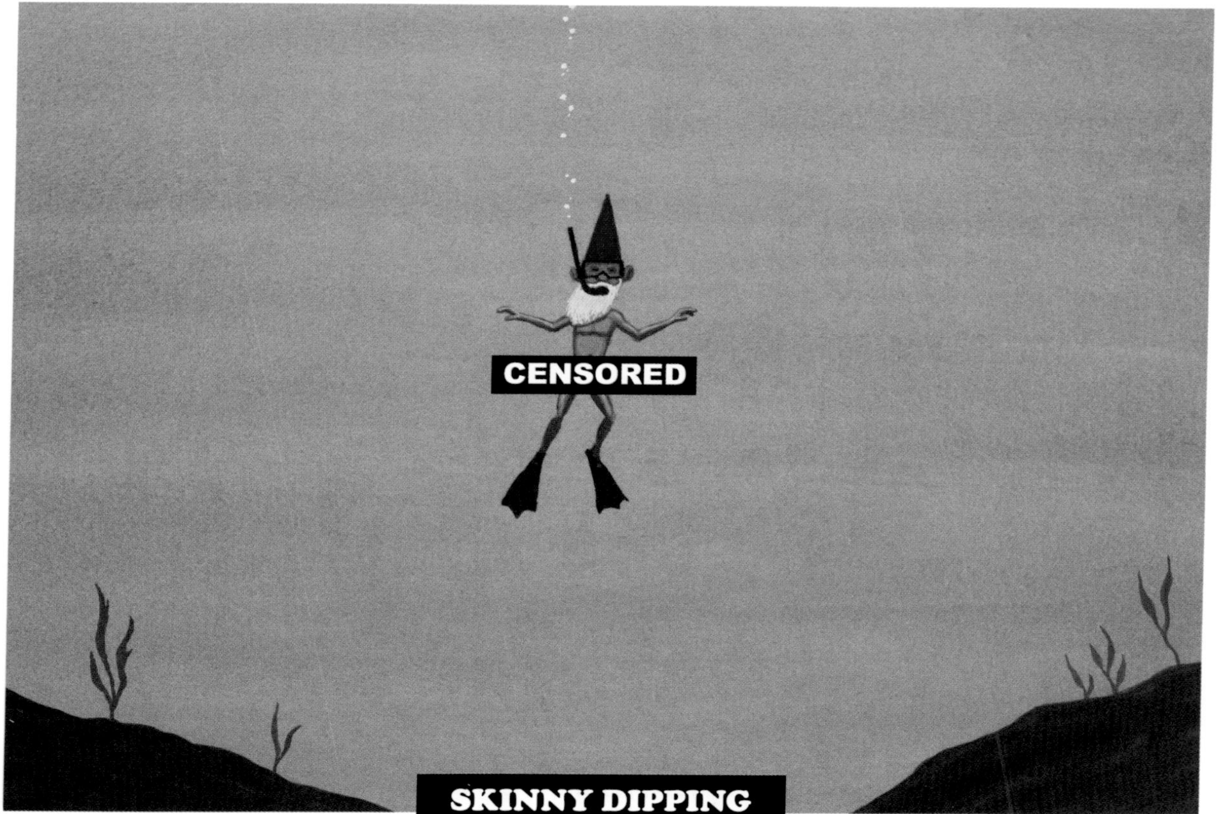
CENSORED

SKINNY DIPPING

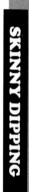

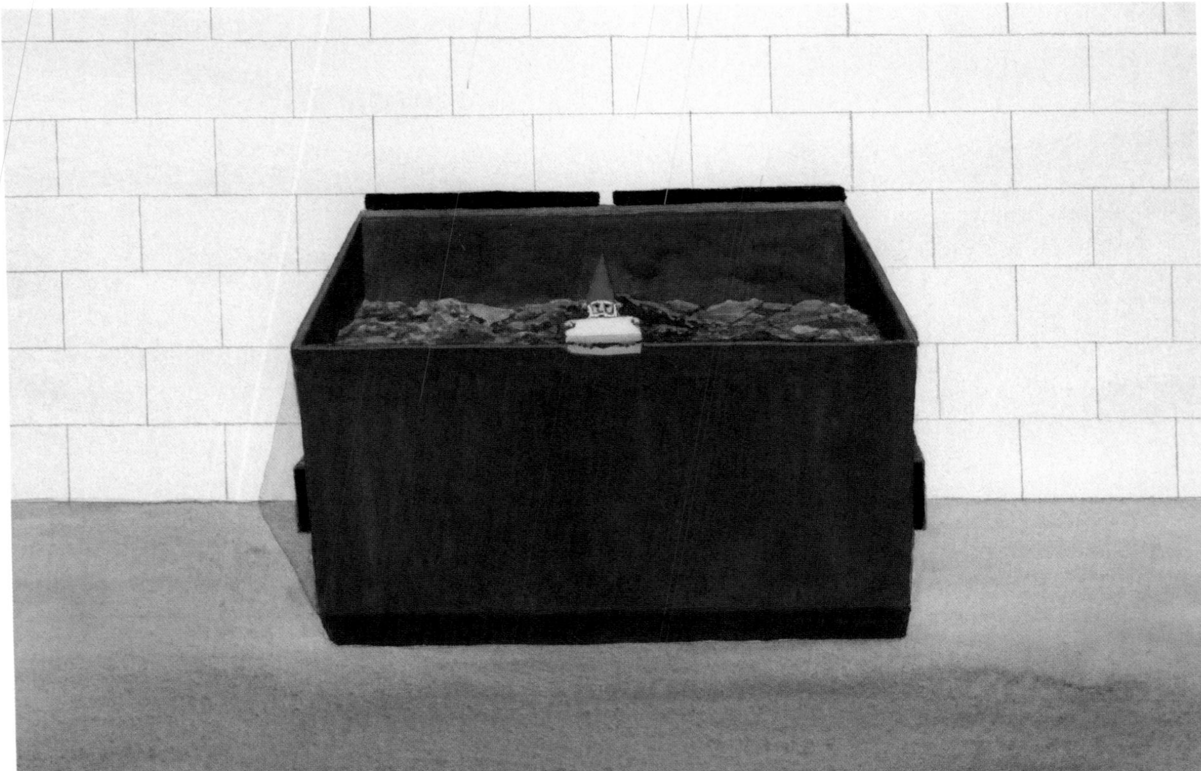

DUMPSTER DIVING

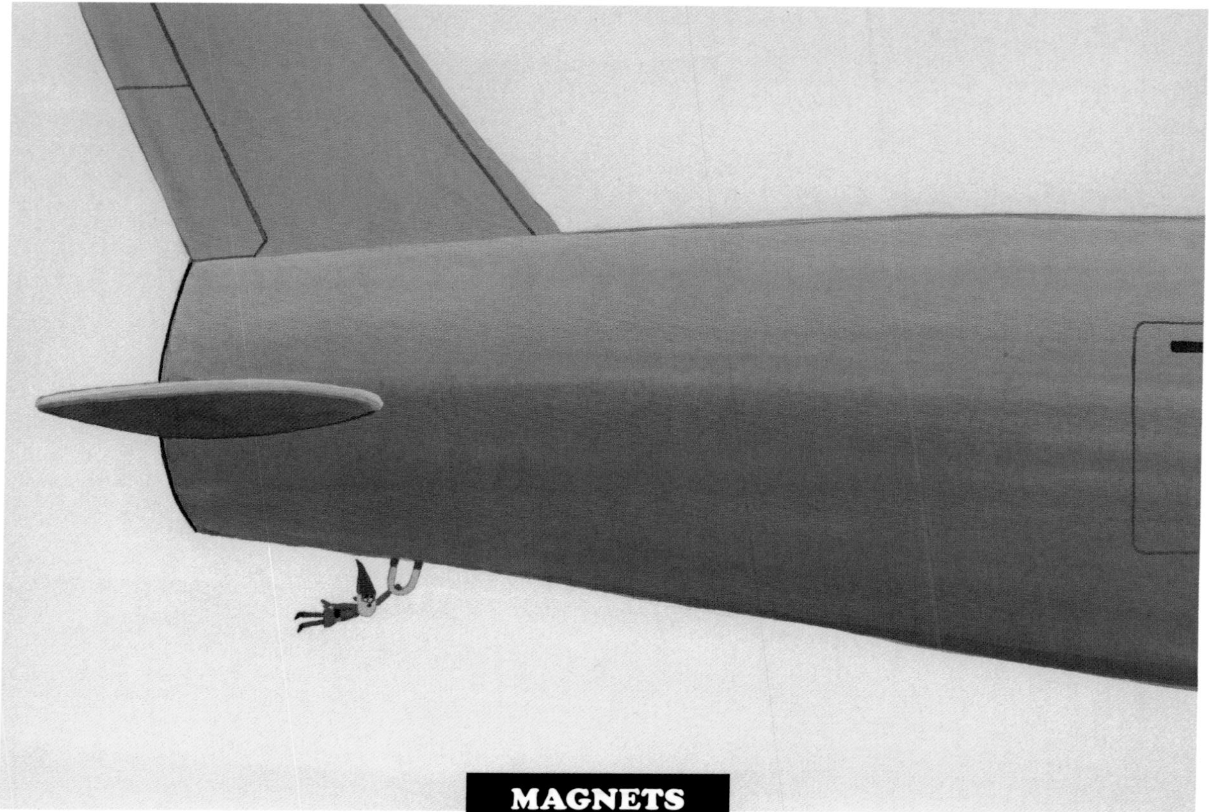

MAGNETS

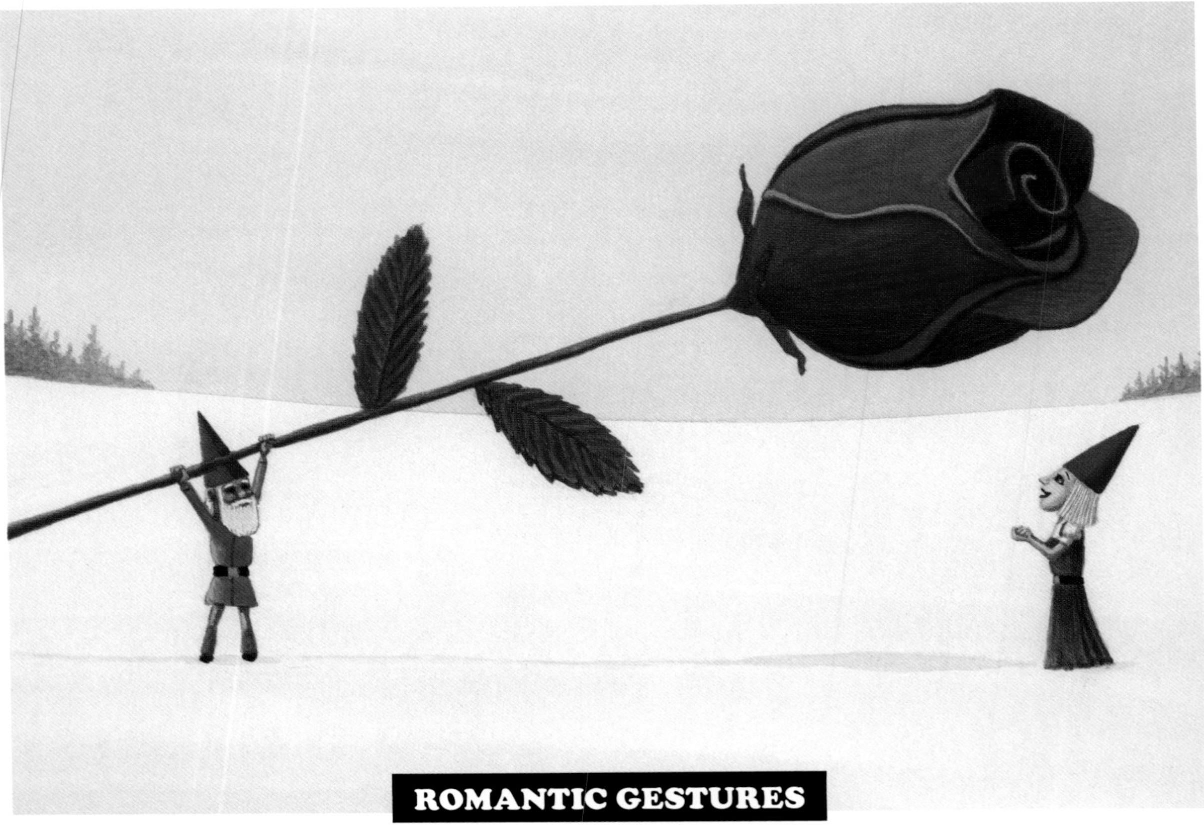

ROMANTIC GESTURES

GARDEN GNOMES HAVE MAJOR ISSUES WITH . . .

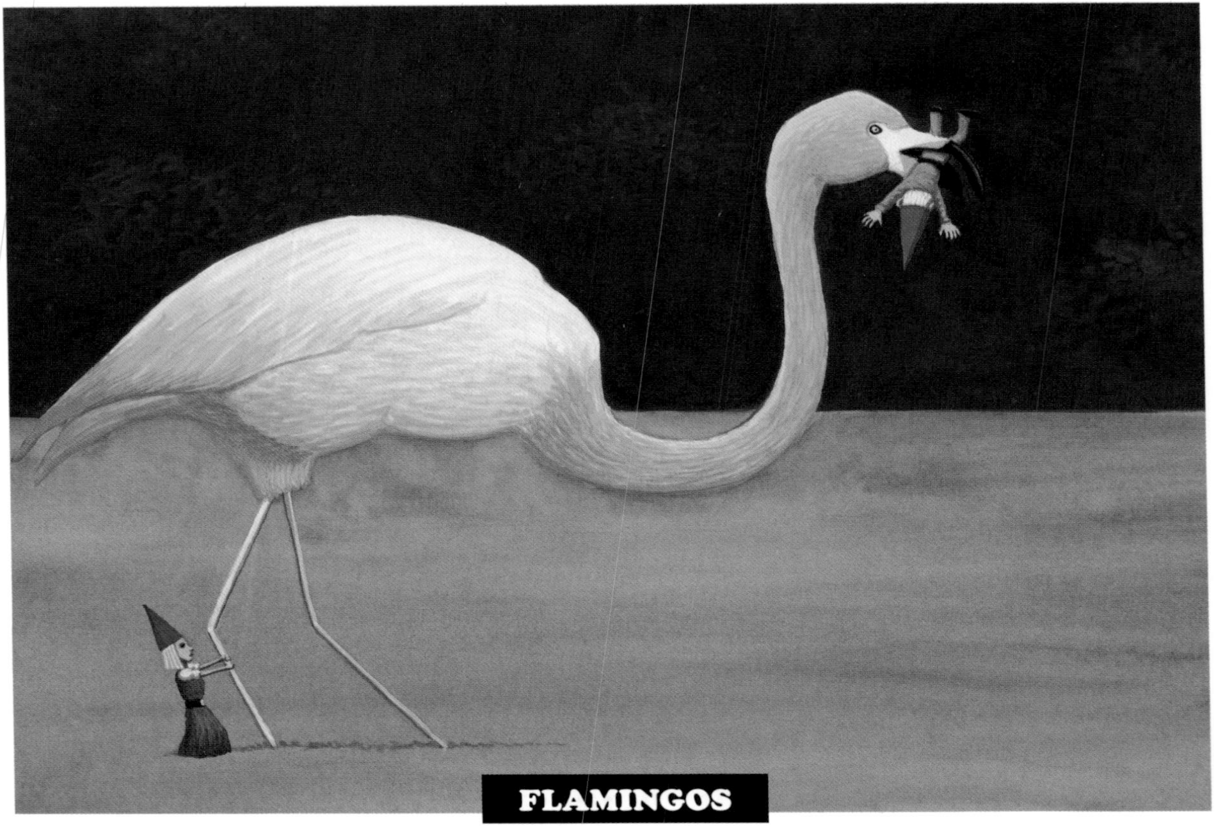

FLAMINGOS

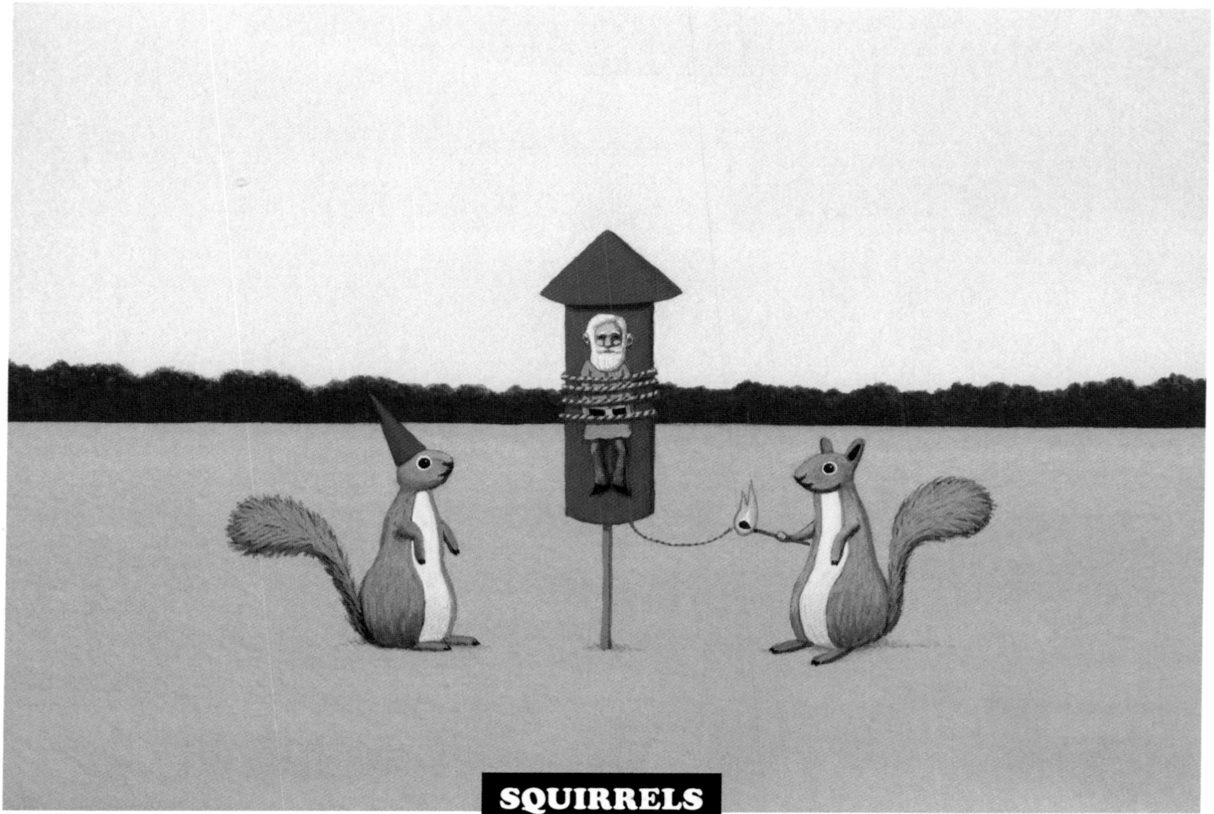

SQUIRRELS

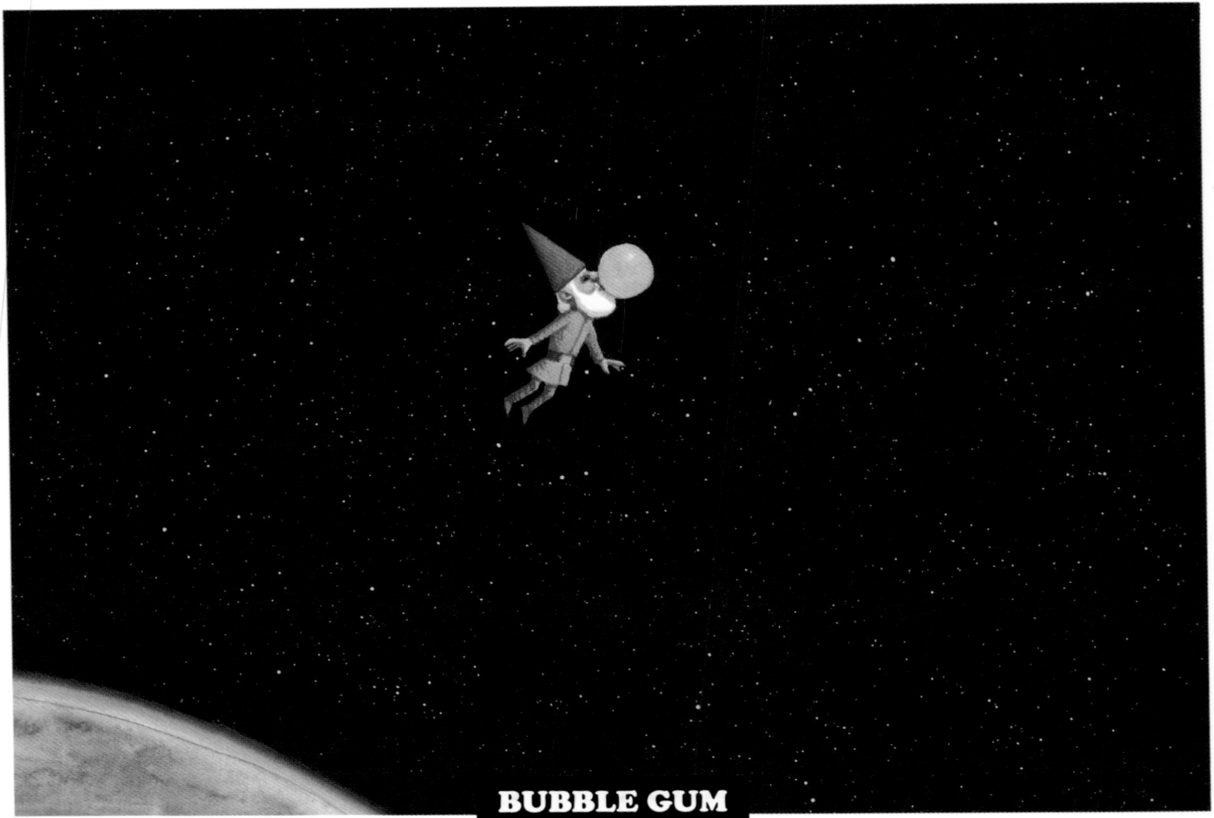

BUBBLE GUM

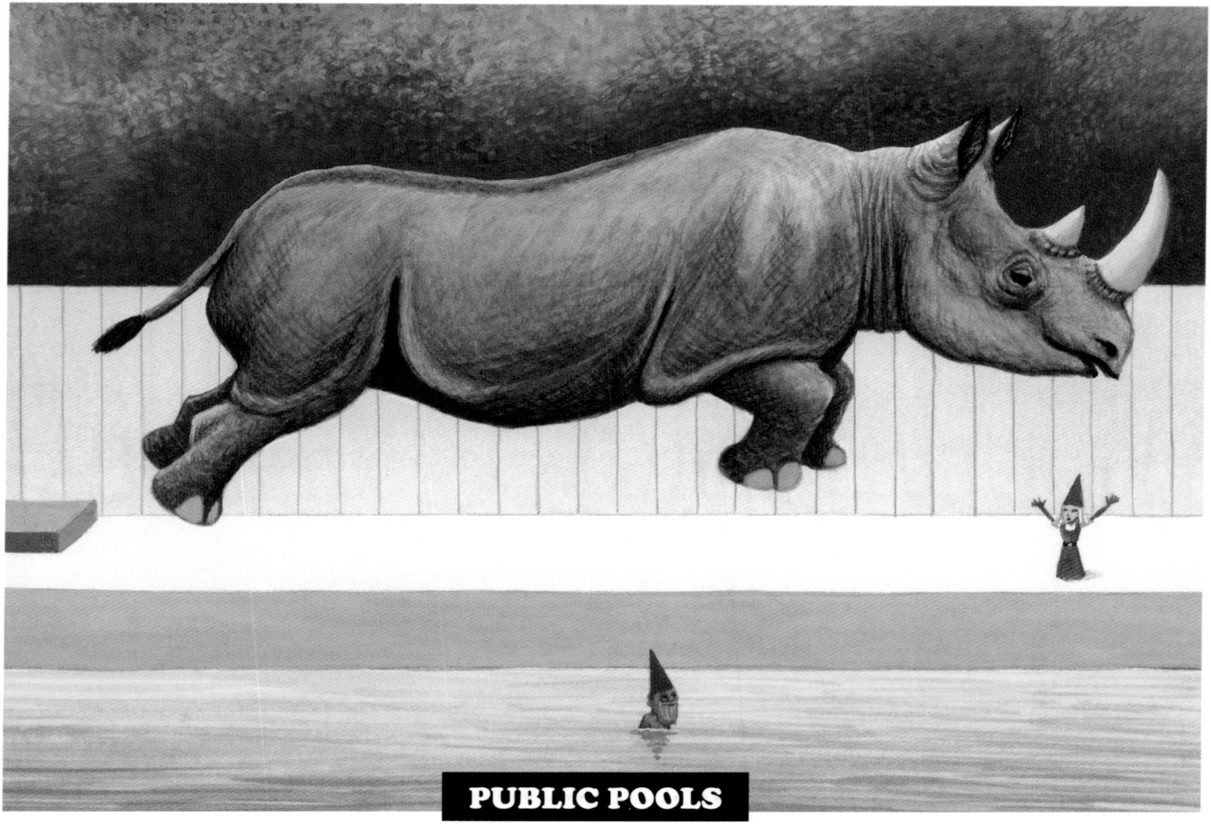

PUBLIC POOLS

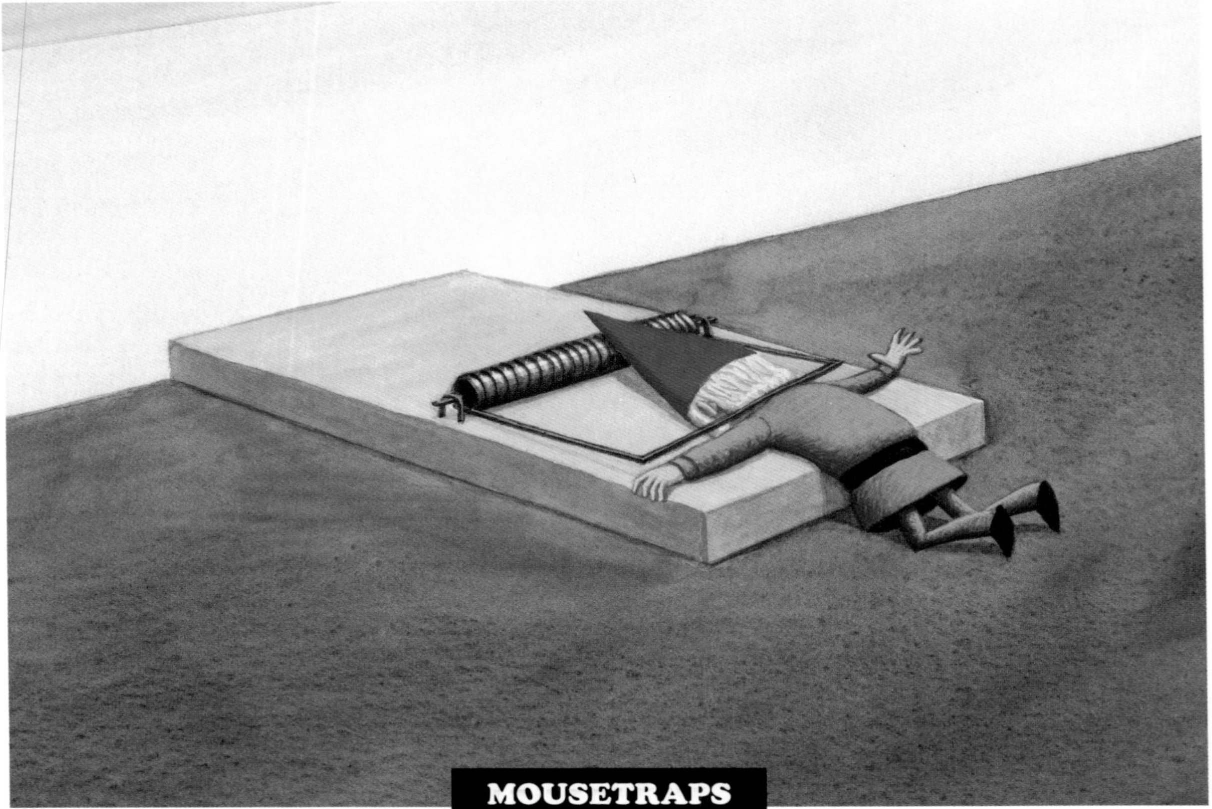

MOUSETRAPS

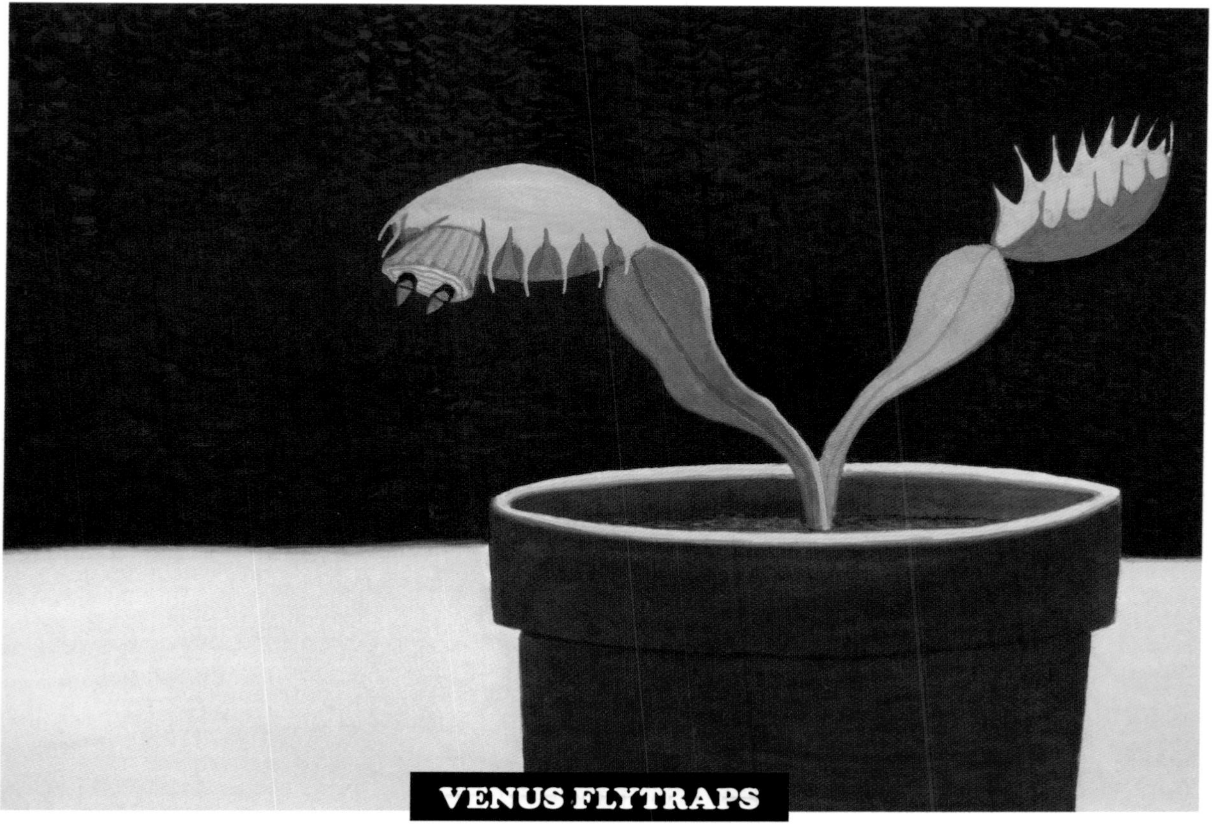

VENUS FLYTRAPS

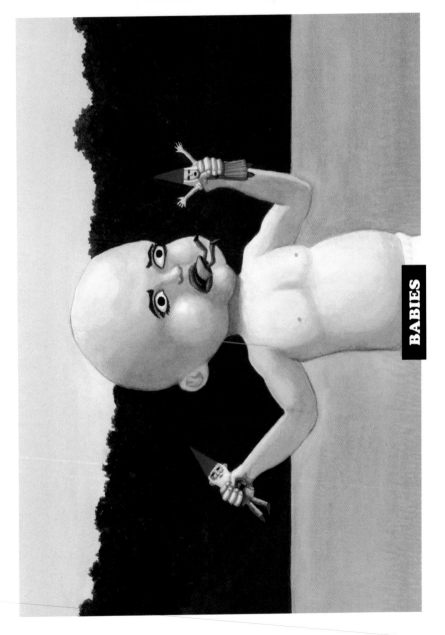

BABIES

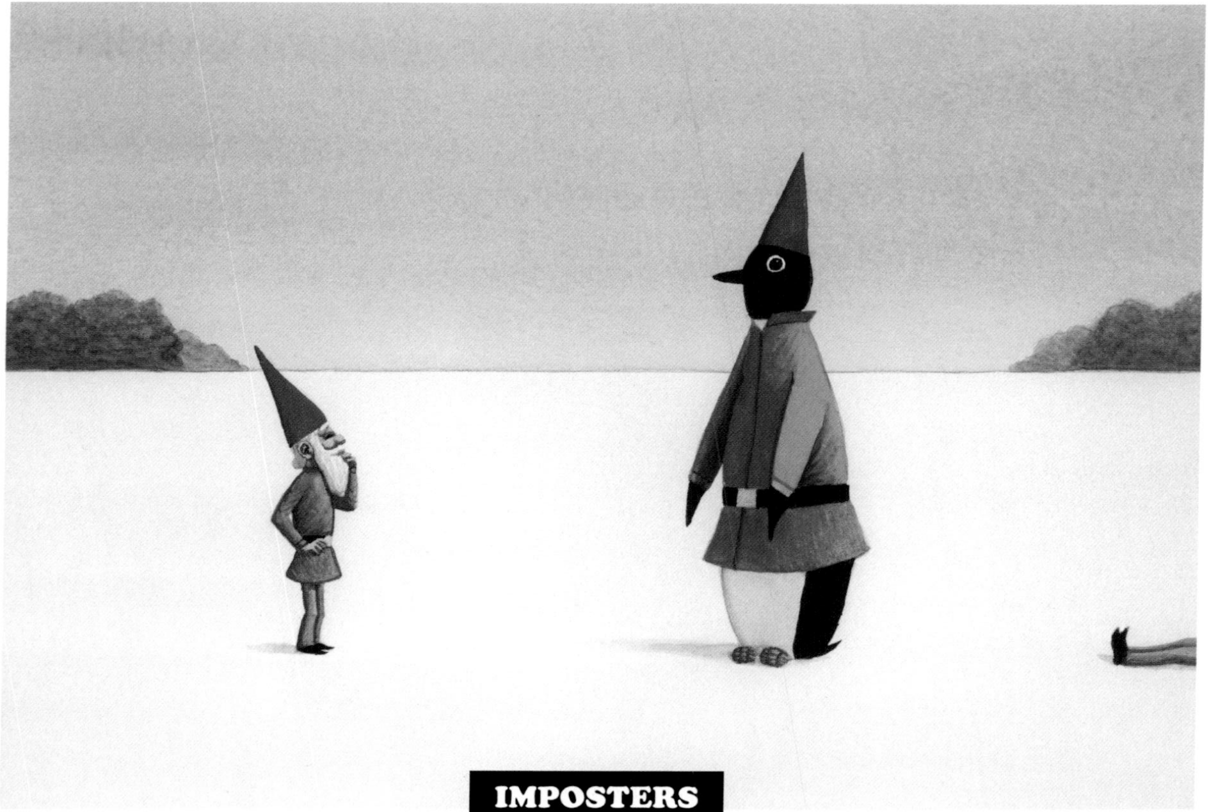

IMPOSTERS

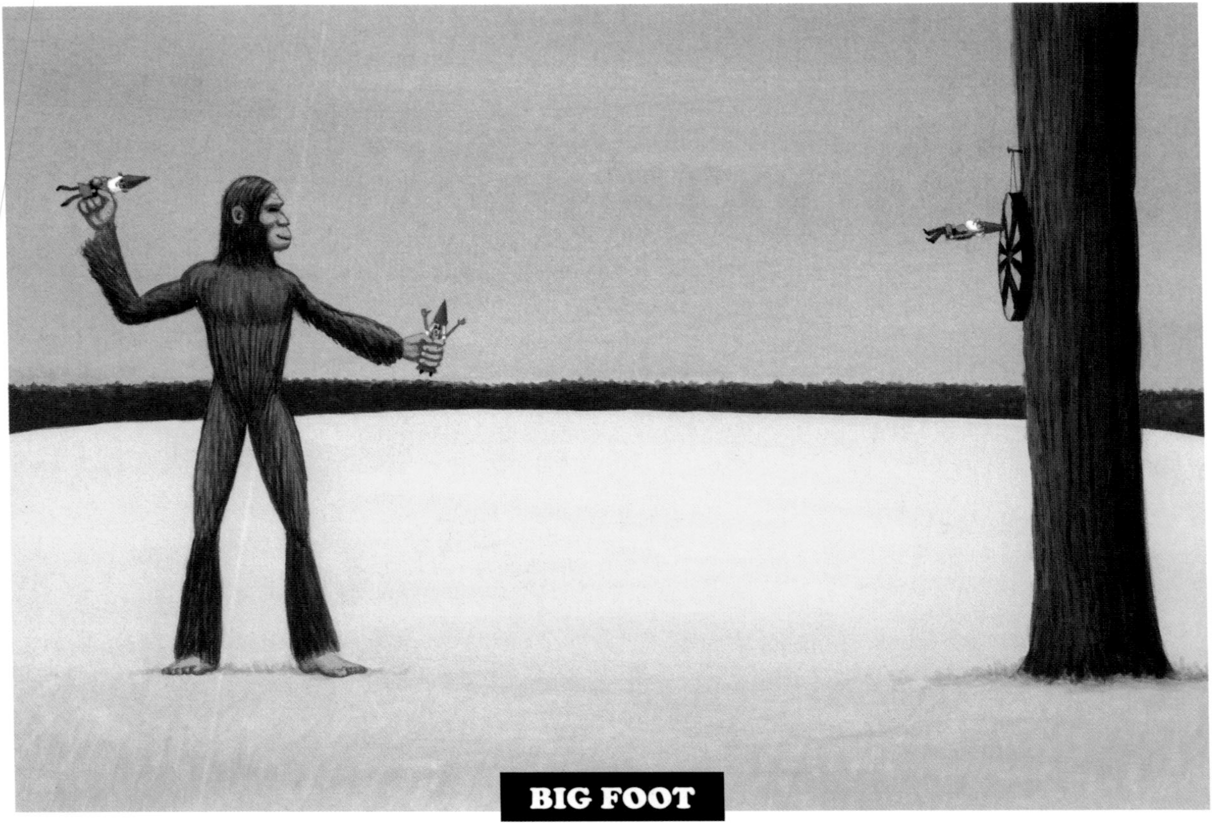

BIG FOOT

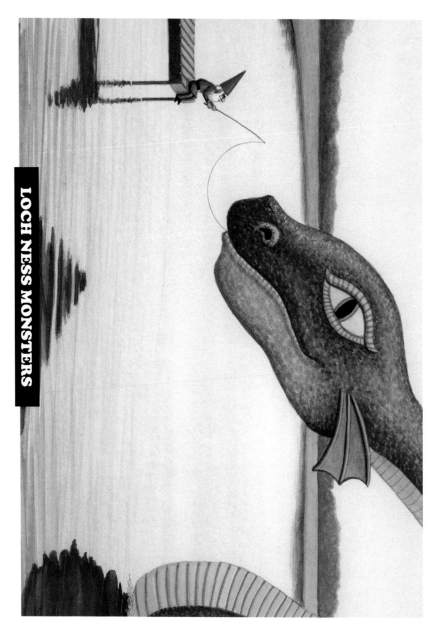

LOCH NESS MONSTERS

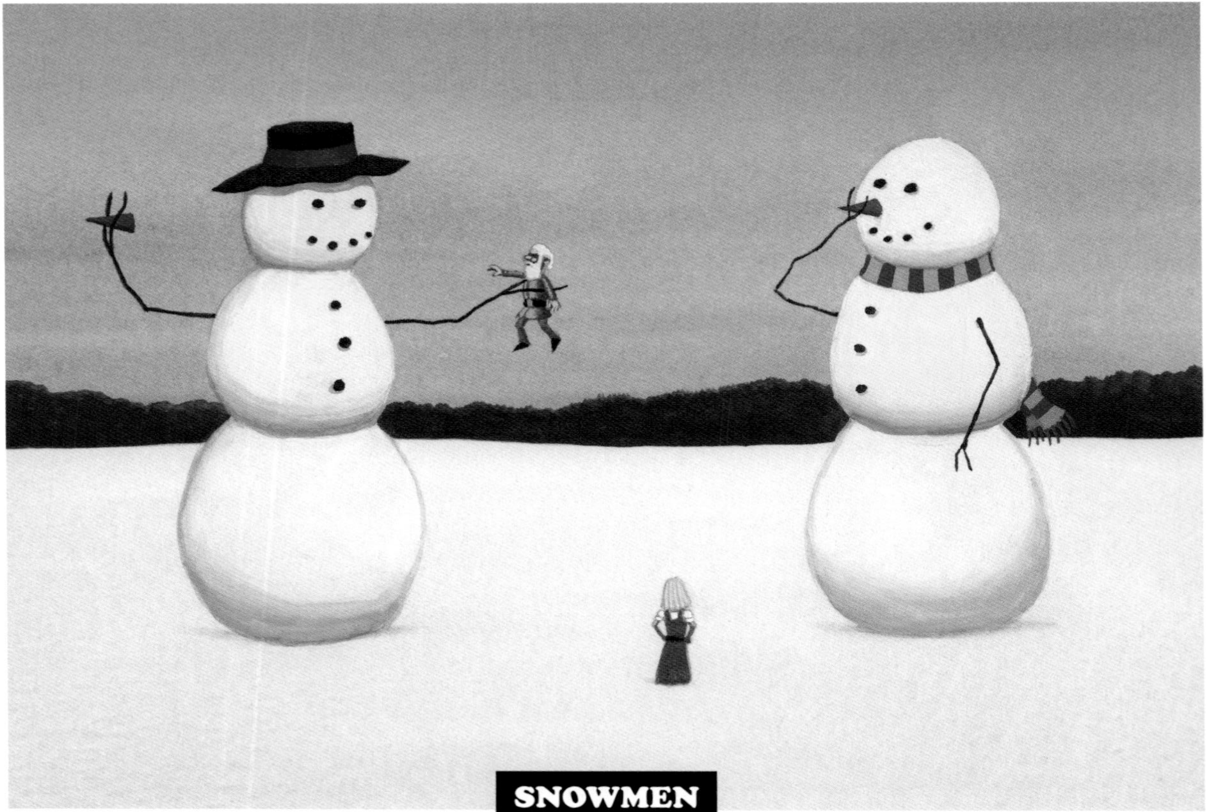

SNOWMEN

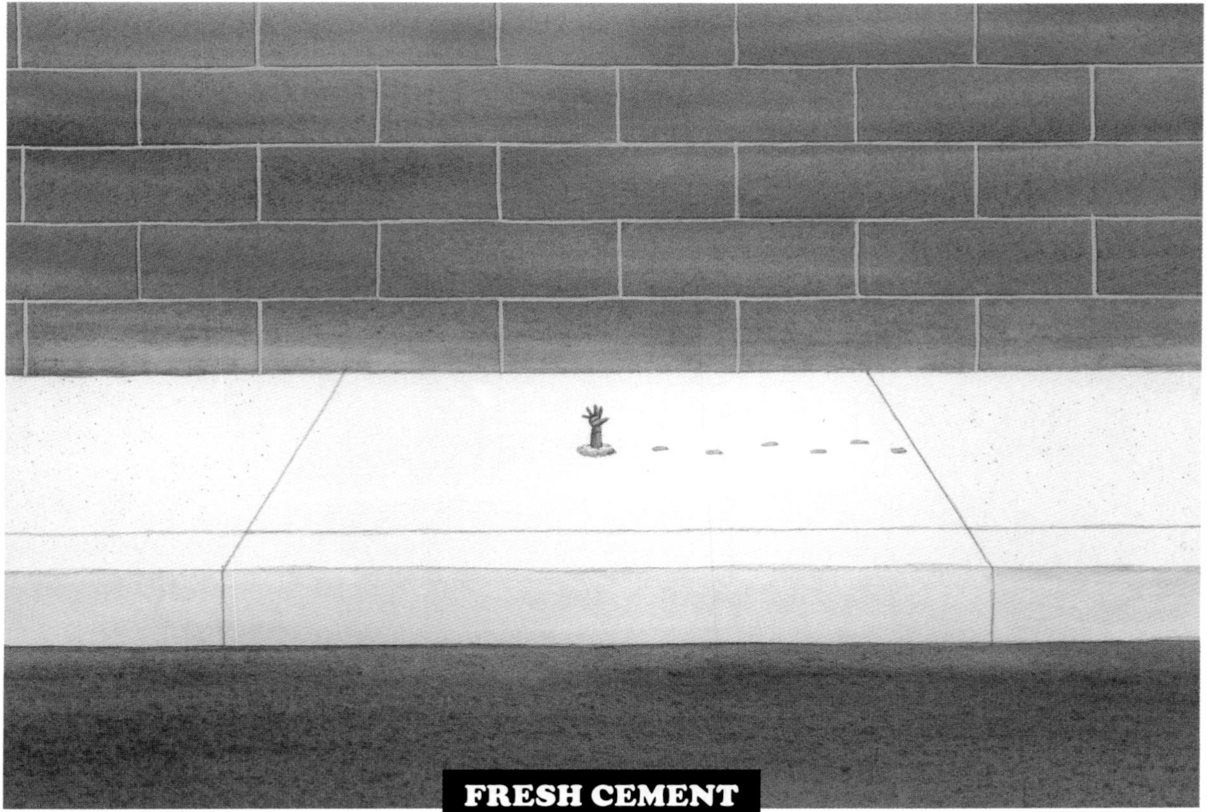

FRESH CEMENT

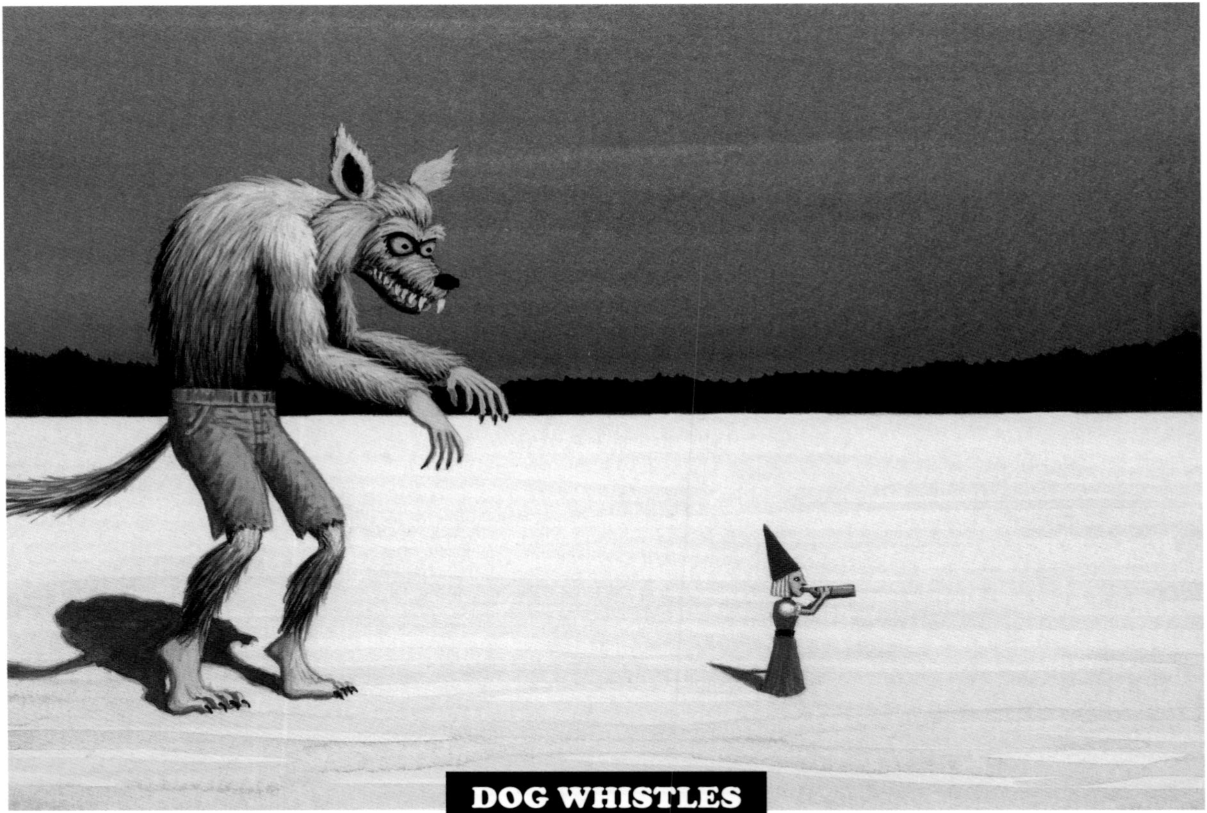

DOG WHISTLES

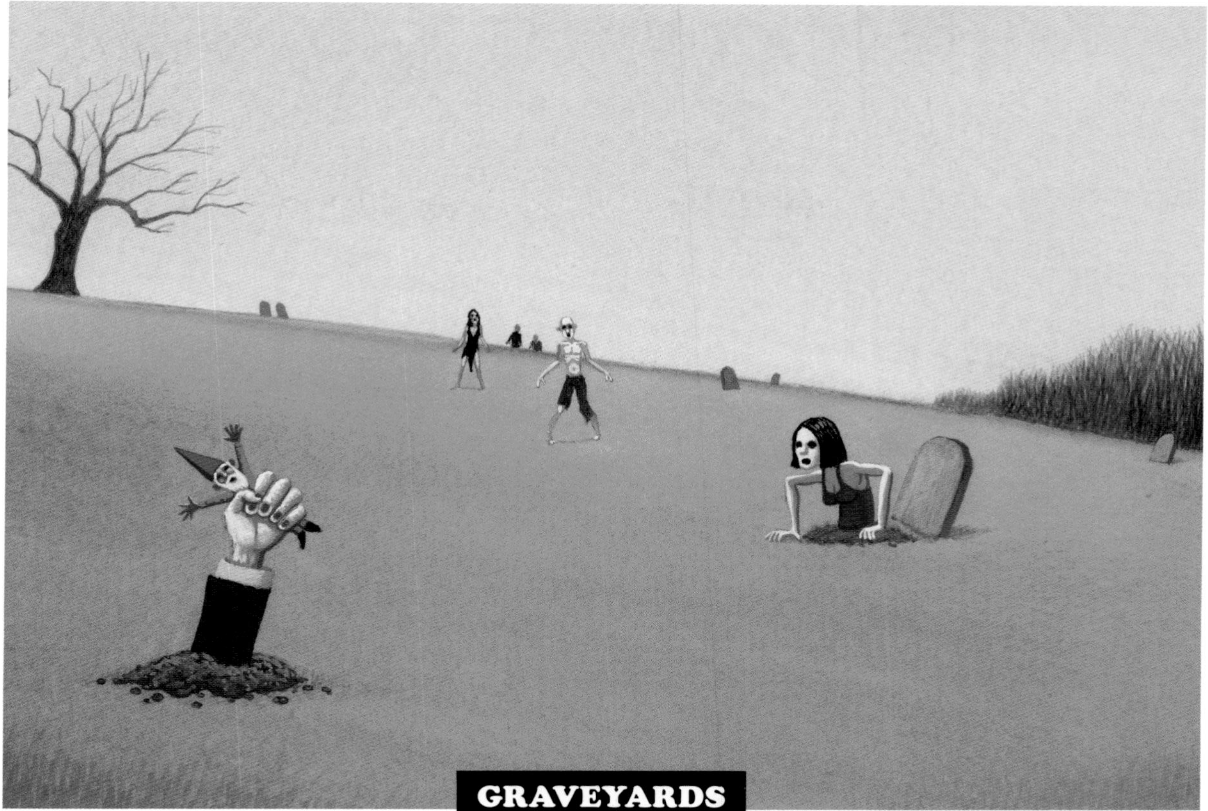

GRAVEYARDS

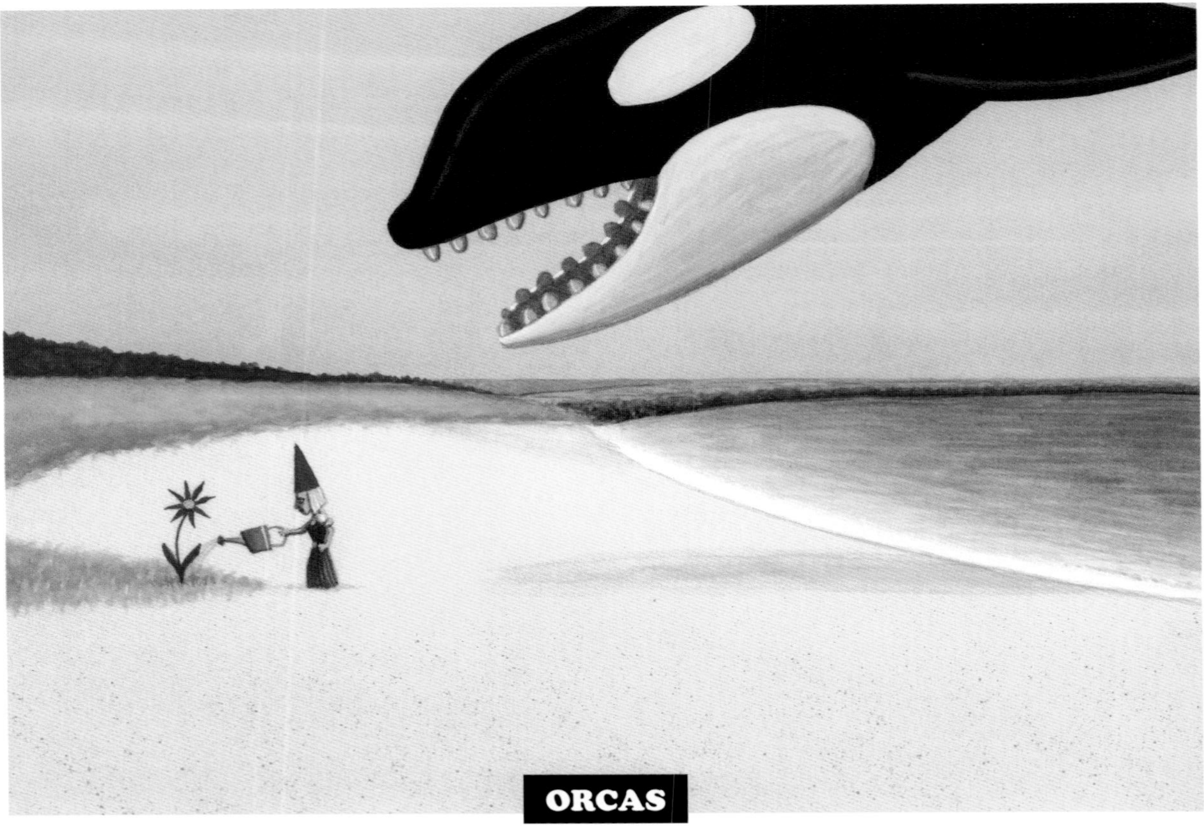
ORCAS

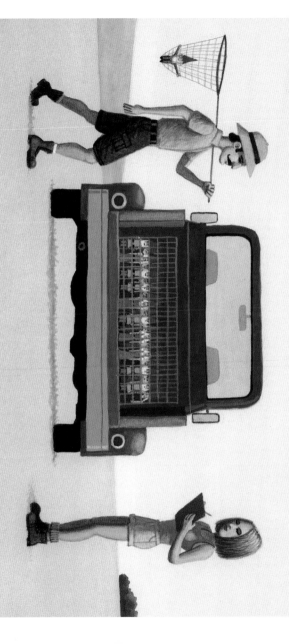

CRYPTOZOOLOGISTS

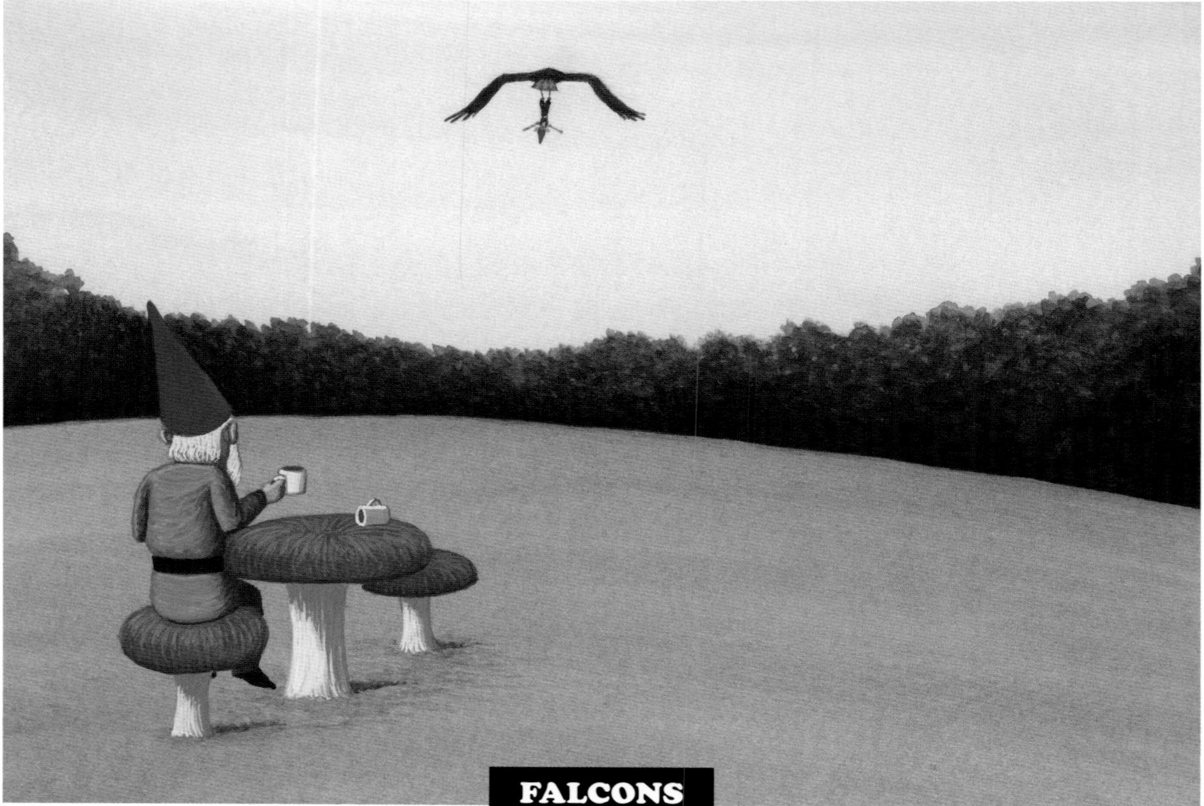

FALCONS

GARDEN GNOMES REALLY LOVE . . .

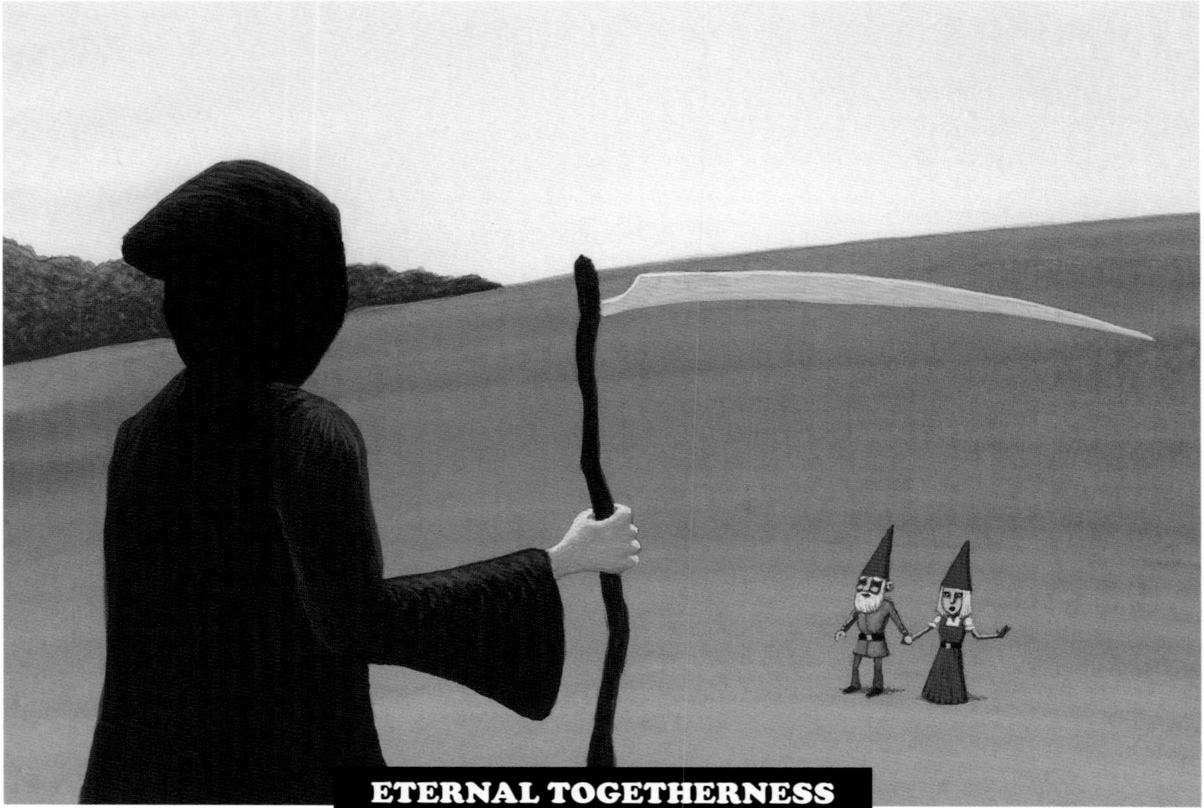

ETERNAL TOGETHERNESS

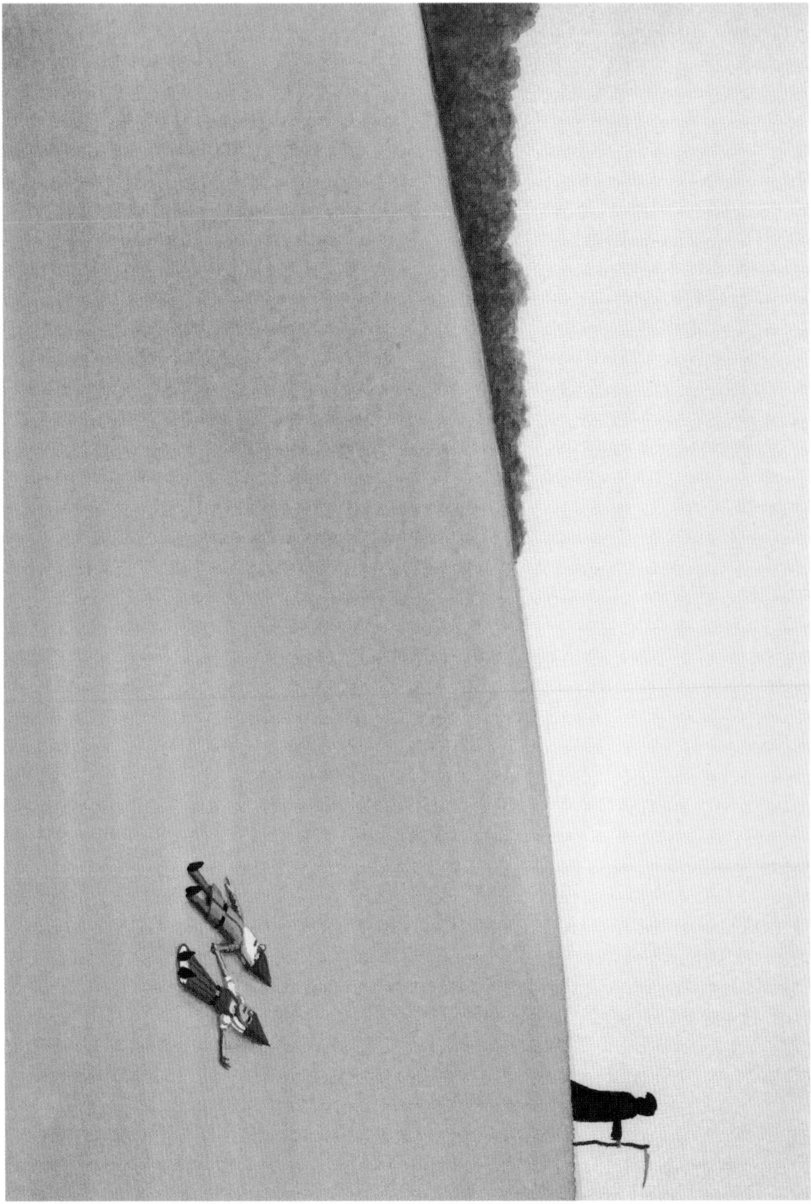

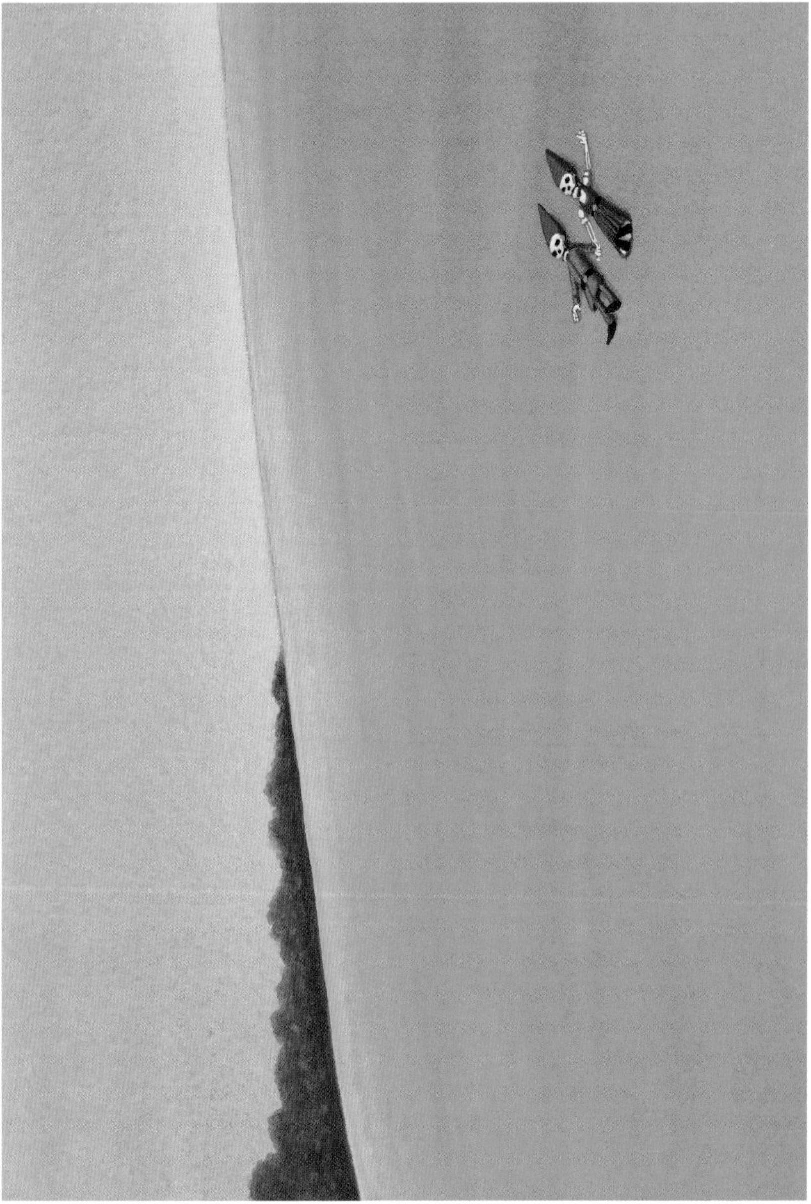

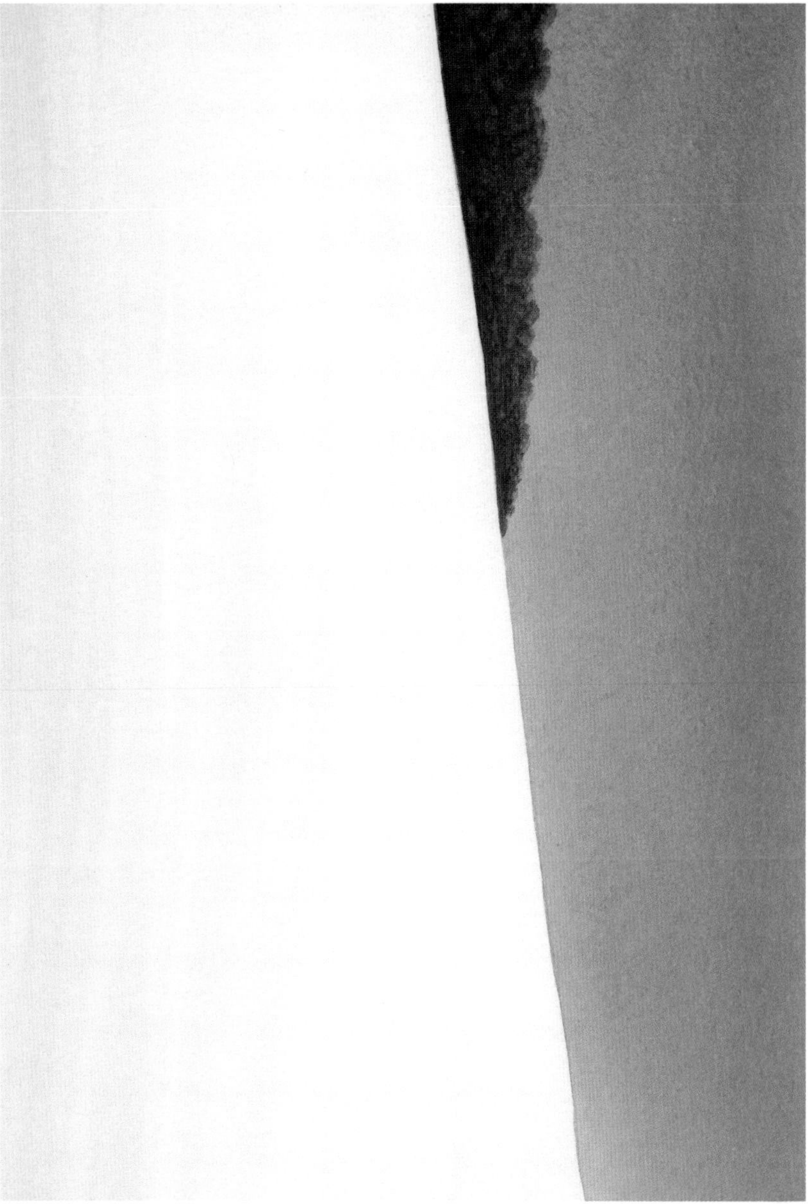

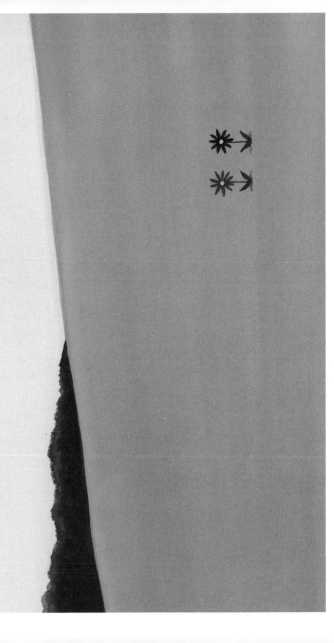